D1588513

HAND COLOURED
FASHION PLATES
1770—1899

PLATE I

"A Peep into Kensington Gardens"
From Heideloff's "Gallery of Fashion," June, 1794

Hand Coloured

FASHION
PLATES

1770 to 1899

by

Vyvyan
Holland

London
B. T. BATSFORD LTD

ISBN 0–7134–6018–0

PRINTED AND BOUND IN GREAT BRITAIN BY
BUTLER & TANNER LTD, FROME AND LONDON
FOR THE PUBLISHERS
B. T. BATSFORD LTD
4 FITZHARDINGE STREET, W1H 0AH

To
My Friend
JAMES LAVER

CONTENTS

ACKNOWLEDGMENTS

M Y grateful thanks are due to James Laver, C.B.E., Keeper of the Departments of Engraving, Illustration and Design, and of Paintings at the Victoria and Albert Museum, London, who provoked me to write this book; to Mrs. Doris Langley Moore, who provided a large number of the fashion-plates in this book and a great deal of valuable advice; to Mrs. William King, whose collection has also supplied me with a considerable number of plates.

I also wish to acknowledge the assistance given to me by the Metropolitan Museum of New York, the British Museum, and Percy Muir, of Messrs Elkin Matthews & Co., Ltd.

SUMMER, 1955   *Vyvyan Holland*

LIST OF ILLUSTRATIONS

15

16

INTRODUCTION

THERE must be very few people with any feeling of artistry in their souls who have not, at one time or another, paused before the window of an antiquarian bookshop in which coloured Victorian fashion-plates are offered for sale. There is something so admirable in the poise of the ladies as they give one another cups of tea or dandle their children or swing miniature croquet mallets at outsize croquet balls. Not a hair, a ruffle or a ribbon out of place, not a wrinkle on their brows, and their feet encased in miniature dolls' shoes which a Chinese lady of the old régime would have found it difficult to wear. And how beautifully their creations seemed to fit them! They seem to be almost part of themselves, and how they ever sat down or ate a meal without disturbing the general arrangement is a mystery. It is of these fashion-plates that this book proposes to deal; of their origin, their evolution and their subsequent decline.

This is not a history of costume. A vast amount of literature already exists on that subject, in many languages. But of the history of fashion-plates and of the publications in which they appeared very little has been written and, indeed, very little is known. Yet it is a fascinating study, because without the existence of these plates it would be almost impossible to study the evolution of costume at all.

What is a fashion-plate? And what is the difference between a fashion-plate and a costume-plate? For there is a wide difference between them. A fashion-plate may be said to be a drawing made for the purpose of showing people the right kind of clothes for them to wear to be abreast of the fashion of the moment; it may also predict what the fashionable person will be wearing in the near future, though this is largely a development which has taken place within the past few years, since French Haute Couture has completely dominated the size, shape and even the gait of the women of the world. It is in this that the fashion-plate differs essentially from the costume-plate, which is intended to show national or theatrical costume, or to put past fashions on record. In fact the fashion-plate speaks for the present or the future, whereas the costume-plate speaks for the past. It is the same as the difference between George Saintsbury's *Notes from a Cellar Book*, in which he recalls the glories of old wines, and the wine-list of a serious wine merchant, which gives a promise of glorious wines to come.

Of course, to a large extent any contemporary portrait of a fashionable woman may be said to be a fashion-plate, in that it shows the clothes worn by the well-dressed woman at the time the portrait was painted. For instance, Winterhalter's picture *l'Impératrice Eugénie et ses Dames d'Honneur* is, in its way, one of the finest fashion-plates of the 1850s. And the most important library of fashion books ever formed, that of Freiherr von Lipperheide, of Berlin, where it is, or was before the war, still preserved, included nearly every topical illustrated periodical produced in European countries, irrespective of whether they contained fashion articles or not. Lipperheide also collected any engraving of any period that showed details of contemporary clothing.

Now this seems to be carrying matters too far, as there can be no possible end to it and it must constitute a whole-time occupation. That is why I have confined myself to engraved or lithographed plates, issued as embellishments to periodicals either wholly or partly devoted to fashion, coloured by hand and appearing in monthly, fortnightly or weekly parts for the delectation and instruction of ladies of discrimination, discretion, wealth and fashion.

Fashion-plates must not be confused with the "trade plates" issued by fashion houses and by manufacturers of dress materials, offering suggestions as to how their silks and satins and cloths can be made up to the best advantage. These are really only advertisements, and I am, therefore, not referring to them. Nor am I touching on periodicals devoted exclusively to masculine dress. The study of masculine fashion magazines is an entirely separate subject, one to which I hope that Mrs. Langley Moore will one day apply herself, as she has promised to do.

22

The reason that I have confined myself to "hand-coloured" plates is that in the nineteenth century there were innumerable magazines published giving pictures of the latest fashions in black and white, and it would be a heart-breaking, if not a back-breaking, task to try to list them all. But by limiting oneself to the coloured plates it is possible to make a reasonably accurate survey of the whole field.

I must also explain why my study stops at the end of the nineteenth century. Colour printing began to creep in at the end of the 1880s and its early efforts were, to say the least of it, experimental. This detrimental process gradually spread, and by the end of the century the colour print and the chromo-lithograph had almost completely superseded the hand-coloured plate, and the charm of the fashion-plate had in great measure departed. Only a few of the more conservative magazines carried the old tradition into the early years of the new century, notably the *Journal des Demoiselles*, which, having started in 1833, was still being published in 1904. For the English magazine, *The Queen*, it may be said that it did not succumb to mechanisation until 1898.

I would have liked to have reproduced all the plates in this book in colour, but this would not have been practicable, owing to the greatly increased cost of colour printing in recent years. By reproducing most of the plates in monochrome it is hoped that the book will come within the reach of everyone who may be interested in the subject.

The covering and adornment of the human body have always been subjects of absorbing interest to mankind. Even the most primitive societies adorn their bodies profusely, particularly for warlike or ceremonial occasions. The men festoon themselves with birds' feathers and the teeth of wild animals and paint themselves in vivid colours, to make themselves look more formidable and to strike terror into the hearts of their enemies; the women adorn their limbs with the scarcest or what they consider to be the prettiest objects to be found in their surroundings, so as to attract the interest and attention of the men. The nature of such adornments tends to conform to a certain pattern, but they vary from tribe

23

to tribe, thus enabling the members of various tribes to distinguish one from the other. And in these adornments we see the prototypes of national and regional costumes of later or higher civilisations.

But national and regional costumes are not subject to much change, if any at all, through the ages. The ancient Greeks, Romans, Assyrians and Egyptians each wore their own distinctive costumes, but they remained approximately the same for centuries; and it is not until the Middle Ages that we become conscious of constantly changing fashion, which at first manifested itself mainly in the matter of head-dresses.

Of the clothes worn by Europeans in pre-Christian and mediæval times we know very little, if anything at all. The illustrators of biblical and classical stories have evolved a conventional costume for their characters, based mainly on the accepted idea of the Roman toga. The few contemporary records that have come down to us are in the form of illuminated books and manuscripts, pottery, sculpture, coins and a certain number of rather crude paintings. Even these mostly portray deities, monarchs, priests or soldiers in their celestial, regal, ceremonial or military attire; so they throw no light on what ordinary men and women wore in the course of their everyday lives. They are hardly more representative of the dress worn by the people of the time than the Court dress of today, to say nothing of the robes of priests and judges and the uniforms of diplomats and of the fighting services, is representative of modern dress.

Although fashion in dress plays such an important part in the contemporary life of any period, it is only during the past fifty years that serious attempts have been made to record its vagaries and to analyse it in its relation to the history of its period. And it is only during still more recent years that organised efforts have been made to preserve examples of contemporary clothing for the instruction and benefit of future generations.

Clothing worn by Queen Victoria and other members of the Royal Family, as well as by Lord Nelson, the Duke of Wellington and even by Lily Langtry, has been on view in various museums for many years, but of the clothing worn by the mass of the people very little remains. People wore their clothes until they went out of fashion or began to show signs of wear; they then handed them over to less fortunate people than themselves, who wore them until they were reduced to rags and were thrown away. It is only by accident that items occasionally turn up in forgotten trunks and wardrobes. When one thinks of the countless millions of articles of clothing that have been worn through the centuries, it seems odd that so few of them have survived, even allowing for the wear and tear of time and the ravages of moths, ladies' maids and other insects! This is a grave misfortune from the point of view of the student of costume, though it is one which, in Great Britain at any rate, Mrs. Doris Langley Moore is doing her best to remedy by forming an extensive Museum of Costume at Eridge Castle, near Tunbridge Wells. Another important collection is the one at Platt Hall, Manchester, formed by Dr. C. Willett Cunnington. Dress is also strongly represented at the Victoria and Albert Museum and at the London Museum, the latter being particularly strong in the Coronation Robes worn by Royalty. In the United States, also, there are several extensive collections of costume, notably in the Costume Institute of the Metropolitan Museum of New York.

However, although so few of the actual clothes worn by our immediate ancestors have come down to us, we are still able to make a careful study of their fashions through the fashion periodicals and fashion-plates that form the subject-matter of this book.

Until the second half of the eighteenth century, a general trend of fashion changes in Europe cannot be said to have existed. The dress worn by men and women was to a great extent regional and its tendencies changed slowly, each nation developing along lines of its own. Before that time artists, in depicting contemporary dress, did so only incidentally, in the course of painting noble or distinguished people; or they confined themselves to showing national costume or the dress worn by people who followed certain trades or callings; and naturally the theatrical profession entered largely into this. It is true that isolated examples of pictures of clothes to be worn on special occasions, particularly Court and wedding dresses, appeared from time to time; but it was not until the seventeenth century that such plates began to be produced with the sole object of showing the clothing worn by persons of taste; even these pictures were still more for the purpose of record than for guidance, and as such do not come into the scope of the present book which, I repeat, does not pretend to be in any way a history of costume or fashion, even within the limits to which it is confined.

However, in studying the evolution of fashion-plates, one cannot ignore their forerunners, the costume-plates of the seventeenth and eighteenth centuries, especially as it is often a little difficult to decide to which of the two categories they belong. So in the next chapter I will deal with these forerunners, and with the steps that led up to the fashion magazines and fashion-plates as they still flourish today.

1 "Spring". Engraved by Richard Gaywood after W. Hollar, 1654.
The corset is an integral part of the costume

3 Lady of Quality strolling incognito in the street. Engraved by F. Ertinger after J. D. de Saint-Jean, 1689

2 "Winter". Engraved by Richard Gaywood after W. Hollar, 1654. The hood and mask are intended to keep out the cold. Note the muff

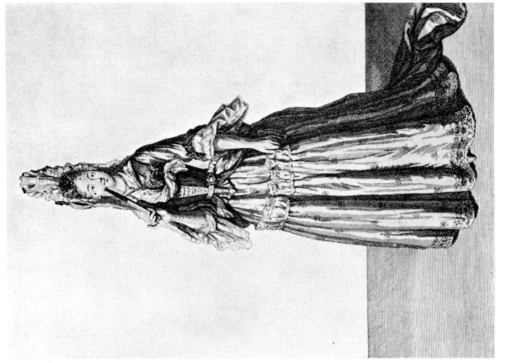

5 Lady of Quality in a steenkerke and furbelow.
By J. D. de Saint-Jean, 1693

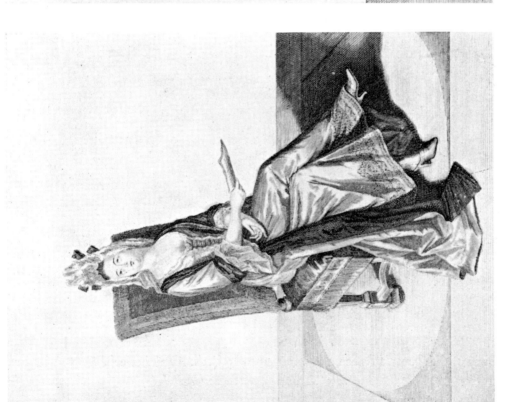

4 Lady of Quality in négligé. By J. D. de Saint-Jean, 1693

6 A Lady of the Queen's Palace, 1777. Engraved by P. A. Martini after Moreau le Jeune
From "Le Monument du Costume"

CHAPTER ONE

The Forerunners : Costume Plates

THE earliest attempts to produce pictures of clothing as such, as distinct from their wearers, were records of national and regional dress. Albrecht Dürer made a series of the costumes of Nuremberg and Venice in 1494. Giacomo Franco produced his series of *Habiti delle Donne Veneziane* in 1610, and Romeyn de Hooghe issued his *Figures de la Mode* in Amsterdam in the same century. These engravings showed what fashionable women were wearing in their respective countries at the time; but they were, I repeat, meant more to be a record of what had been worn in the immediate past than for instruction as to what to wear in the future.

Apart from these and a few other isolated cases of artists travelling abroad and painting the costumes of the countries they visited, very few attempts were made to record contemporary costume until the seventeenth century, in which a considerable number of costume-plates appeared. Even then these plates were issued spasmodically, one or two at a time, and were produced more for education or amusement, or to satisfy curiosity, than to attempt to predict future fashions. As Mr. James Laver succinctly puts it, they were "intended more for rapportage than for prophecy". It should be noted that at first these plates were mostly of male costume and that it was only with the efflux of time that more and more feminine costumes came into the pictures. The reason for this is probably because in those days the clothing of men was much more picturesque than that of women, man's elaborate decoration of his person being really a form of display before the female, in the same way as certain birds "posture" before their prospective mates in the courting season. Actually, in the middle of the eighteenth century, women's clothes became

31

more decorative than those of men, but it was not until after the Napoleonic Wars that European men adopted the drab clothing that they still wear to this day. Efforts are being continually made to redecorate the male, but this is always strenuously resisted by women, who subconsciously dread the competition with which they might have to contend from the more gorgeous male of the species.

The first person to take the drawing of costumes really seriously was Wenceslas Hollar, a Polish artist who was born in Prague in 1607. In spite of strong parental opposition, he adopted art as his profession and subsequently became famous as a draughtsman and an engraver.

Hollar studied in Prague under Matthew Merian, a well-known engraver of the period, but the main influence on his art was the work of Albrecht Dürer. After various vicissitudes which took him to Frankfort, Cologne and Antwerp, where he found it difficult enough to exist, in 1636 he attracted the attention of Thomas Howard, Earl of Arundel, who was at that time English ambassador to the German Emperor. Lord Arundel was so impressed with Hollar's work that he brought him back to England with him in his suite. He now entered upon a period of success and married, according to John Aubrey, the antiquary, "at Arundel House my lady's waiting-woman, by whom he had a daughter, that was one of the greatest beauties that I have seen; his son by her died in the plague, an ingenious youth who drew delicately".

Hollar may be said to be the father of the fashion-plate, or at least its most important ancestor. His first series of costume-plates appeared in London in 1640 and was entitled *Ornatus Muliebris Anglicanus, or the Several Habits of English Women from the Nobilitie to the Country Woman, as they are in these Times*. This series contained twenty-six plates representing mostly the daily wear of the English middle classes; as such, these plates are invaluable to the student of costume. They show female figures, some front or side view and some even back view, and they enter into the most minute details of dress.

In 1643 appeared Hollar's *Theatrum Muliebrum, sive Varietas atque Differentia Habituum Foeminei Sexus*. All titles of books and of series of engravings were long and rather turgid in those days. This work, which was also published in London, consisted of forty-eight plates and gave the different styles of feminine costume in all the principal European countries. Hollar produced other series of costume engravings under such titles as *Runde Frauentracht* (1644, thirty-seven plates) and *Aula Veneris* (*ca.* 1650). He also published a remarkable series of etchings of costume accessories such as muffs, fans, aprons, watches, *nécessaires* or *châtelaines* and, of course, hats. Reticules, or handbags, had not yet made their appearance and were not, indeed, to appear for another hundred years, when women's clothes became so flimsy that it was not practical to add pockets to them.

Poor Hollar suffered from the troubles of the times in which he lived. The Puritan Revolution in England drove him back to Holland, where he worked for a niggardly wage, marked out by an hour-glass at fourpence an hour; and in the course of these labours he produced some of his best work. In all he designed 2740 plates on various subjects; he died in 1677, in his seventieth year, in straitened circumstances. Of him John Aubrey, who was a friend of his, wrote: "He was a friendly, good-natured man as could be, but shiftless as to the world, and died not rich." John Evelyn, the diarist, tells us that he was a very honest, simple, well-meaning man. Bénézit, in his *Dictionnaire de Peintres, etc.*, sums him up as "a very talented engraver, who was the victim of the events among which he lived".

Figures 1 and 2 are good examples of Hollar's work. They are from the series entitled "The Four Seasons", engraved by Richard Gaywood after Hollar's drawings, and represent Spring and Winter. "Spring" is wearing a semi-transparent collar over her *décolletage*, and carries a posy of flowers in her hand. "Winter" wears a hood and mask, possibly to keep out the cold, though later generations used to cover the chin rather than the eyes to achieve this. The backgrounds are typical; Hollar always put his ladies in such rather elaborate settings.

Later in the seventeenth century several other artists came into the field of the costume-plate, and something must be said about their work, as they also belong essentially to the ancestry of the fashion-plate.

Foremost among these artists was Jean Dieu de Saint-Jean, about whom, unfortunately, little is known except that he was a prolific designer and engraver of costume-plates in the 1660s '70s and '80s. Bénézit devotes only two lines to him, whereas Thieme and Becker in their vast work *Der Allgemeiner Künstlerlexicon* (General Dictionary of Artists) in 37 volumes do not mention him at all; yet there is an outstanding quality in his work that cannot be ignored. A proportion of his plates still depicts regional costumes and uniforms, but a great many of them show the costume of ordinary people engaged in the ordinary occupations of every-day life. One has only to consider the titles of his plates to realise this. Such as *Suit worn with a Sword, Man of Quality in Winter Dress* (1678), *Lady in Town Dress, Lady Singing from a Book of Music, Lady in Morning Déshabille* (1683), *Lady in Summer Déshabille, Man of Quality in a Surtout* (1684), and *Lady Walking in the Country*. For examples of Saint-Jean's work see Figures 3, 4 and 5.

Next in order comes the Bonnart family of engraver-printsellers. There were several of these Bonnarts, and some confusion exists as to the precise relationship between them; but they all contributed to the plates that bear their name. The first generation consisted of four brothers: Nicolas (1636–1718), Henri (1642–1711), Robert (1652–1729) and Jean-Baptiste (1654–1726). Nicolas had a son, also named Nicolas and with whom he is sometimes confused; he was born in 1689 and died in 1762 at the age of 73. And Henri had a son, Jean-Baptiste-Henri (1678–1726), who is sometimes confused with his uncle Jean-Baptiste, who also died in 1726.

However this may be, they are all grouped together under the name of Les Frères Bonnart, the most productive of them being the elder Nicolas. They engraved chiefly male costumes, though they also produced a number of female plates.

Other well-known seventeenth-century costume-plate engravers were Antoine Trouvain (1656–1708), J. Valk, another printseller of whom nothing is known, and Nicolas Arnoult, who flourished in Paris at the end of the century and produced some really delightful plates. One plate of Arnoult's, called *La Charmante Tabagie*, engraved in about 1698, shows three ladies of high quality engaged in smoking clay pipes out of doors, beneath what appears to be a pergola. Arnoult's best-known plate, which has been reproduced many times, is *The French Tailor* (1697), which shows a lady, chaperoned by her maid, having the sleeves of a new garment adjusted.

There were, of course, other artists who occasionally produced costume-plates during this period, but the ones I have mentioned were the more important of them.

The early part of the eighteenth century was singularly deficient in costume-plates, though the Bonnart family were still flourishing and producing plates in the 1730s. Then occurred a hiatus until the last quarter of the century, bridged only by numerous almanacs into which small engravings of female costume were frequently inserted.

Then between 1775 and 1783 appeared the magnificent *Suite d'Estampes pour servir à l'Histoire des Modes et du Costume des François dans le XVIIIe Siècle.** There have been frequent reprints of these plates, which are certainly the best known of all the eighteenth-century costume-plates. But they are still, as their title indicates, only of historical interest, and can in no way be described as fashion-plates. However, from this period onwards we begin to get the real contemporary fashion-plate designed to guide ladies in the choice of their dress.

---

* This series of thirty-six engravings after Freudenberg and Moreau le Jeune was issued in three parts of twelve plates each, appearing respectively in 1775, 1777 and 1783 It is usually known by the shorter title of *Le Monument du Costume*. The plates were engraved by no less than twenty-one different artists. An example is reproduced here in Figure 6.

CHAPTER TWO

The Connecting Links

AT the beginning of 1778 two young printsellers in Paris, named Jacques Esnauts and Michel Rapilly, conceived the idea of issuing coloured prints of the prevailing male and female fashions of the day. Until that time, as we have seen, very little had been attempted in that direction; a few fashion-plates had been issued by periodicals like *The Lady's Magazine*,* published in London, which showed contemporary fashions, but they were not issued in colour, and copies which turn up with the plates coloured were probably embellished by the purchasers in their own homes. Esnauts and Rapilly were, however, more ambitious, and they started issuing a series of coloured fashion-plates under the title of *La Gallerie des Modes*. The exact number of plates issued is not precisely known; they appeared at irregular intervals, in parts consisting of about twenty-four plates to each part, and four parts to a volume, five volumes appearing in all. The title-page of the first volume, which was probably printed when the first volume was complete, described the work as: *Gallerie des Modes et des Costumes Français Dessinés d'après Nature, Gravés par les plus Célébres Artistes de ce Genre, et colorés avec le plus Grand Soin par Madame Le Beau.*

This publication and Heideloff's *Gallery of Fashion*, of which more later in this chapter, were the real connecting links between the costume-plate, as exemplified by the *Monument du Costume*, and the true fashion-plate. The *Gallerie des Modes* was by no means an exclusively fashion periodical, as, interspersed with the fashion-plates, were portraits of leading persons at the French Court and plates showing stage costumes; but it

* The title of this publication varied. It was sometimes called *The Lady's Magazine* and sometimes *The Ladies' Magazine*. I have kept throughout to the title *The Lady's Magazine*, which was that of the first issue.

broke fresh ground in that all the clothes worn were very carefully described, often with amusing details and comments, some of them being far from flattering and declaring them to be very unbecoming; indeed many of the descriptions were taken from contemporary newspapers protesting how unattractive the dresses were.

The *Gallerie des Modes* continued until 1787, when it abruptly ceased. In all it published at least 342 plates, of which only eighteen showed more than one figure; in addition to these there were about seventy-two plates depicting hats, which had at that time reached the height of absurdity for all time. Each of the five volumes had a different allegorical title-page.

This work is extremely scarce. There is no copy in either the British Museum or the Victoria and Albert Museum. Indeed I do not know of any copy, however incomplete, in the British Isles. The only copy in the Bibliothèque Nationale in Paris lacks a number of known plates. The famous Lipperheide collection in Berlin contained 130 of the plates. In fact it is very doubtful whether a complete set of all the plates exists in one place, though doubtless a set could be made up from various sources. The main reason for this is that the plates were not kept together, but were treated as pictures and framed and hung on walls.

There is, however, an elaborately produced reproduction of the work, published in Paris by Émile Lévy in five large folio volumes between 1911 and 1914. The difference between the originals and the reproductions can only be detected (apart from the modern paper on which the reproductions are printed) by very careful line-for-line comparison between them. The reproductions were coloured by hand, as were the originals. The hat plates were omitted, but 325 of the known 342 plates are given.

Some idea of the rarity of the *Gallerie des Modes* may be gathered from some of the prices paid for it at auction in the past. In 1880 a copy lacking eight plates fetched £272. A year or two later a copy consisting of the first two volumes only, containing 147 plates, fetched £232, and in 1909, volume I only, lacking ten plates, fetched about £200. And even the 1911 Lévy reproduction fetches something like £300 when it comes up for sale, which it seldom does; the Victoria and Albert Museum is fortunate in having a copy of this reproduction in its library.

As I have already mentioned, the colouring of the plates was done by hand, on the title-page of the first volume it was announced that this was the work of Madame Le Beau. Nothing is known of this lady, nor is it known how long she went on colouring the plates. Her name does not appear on the title-page of volume II, so we may presume that it was not for very long. We know, too, that the plates were also issued uncoloured. The actual colouring varies very much in execution, and sometimes does not even tally, in certain examples, with the colours given in the descriptive letterpress; copies of the same plate may, indeed, be found in quite different colours.

Four artists were responsible for nearly all the fashion-plates in the *Gallerie des Modes*; there were other contributors, but they are of no real importance.

The first four of these was Claude-Louis Desrais, whose reputation up to that time was that of an etcher of "gallant" illustrations to contemporary novelettes. Desrais is responsible for the first sixty-eight plates in this series, and some of the most charming. He seems to have left the employ of Esnauts and Rapilly in 1780, but to have returned in 1786.

Desrais was followed in 1780 by Pierre-Thomas Leclère. Leclère's designs may not possess the skill or the grace of those of Desrais, but he was so careful to imitate Desrais' style that it is often difficult to distinguish between the work of the two artists.

In 1781 François-Louis-Joseph Watteau joined the staff of the *Gallerie*, but he did not become a regular contributor until after Leclère left in 1783. Watteau was a member of the famous family of artists of that name, and he brought a new note of elegance into the series. His drawings are less mannered than those of Desrais and Leclère and are easily distinguishable from them. His figures are often very much out of proportion, but they are not the less elegant for that. In a plate that I have before me the lady's anatomy consists of one-tenth head, two-tenths body and seven-tenths legs! And yet the whole effect is by no means unpleasing.

The fourth contributor was Augustin de Saint-Aubin, who in 1786 and 1787 contributed eighteen "grandes Robes de Cour à l'Etiquette". I think that the nearest translation of this into English would be "Court Dresses for State Occasions".

In the eighteenth century, and indeed in the first decade of the nine-

7   Mantelet à Coulisses. By Claude-Louis Desrais
From "La Gallerie des Modes," 1778

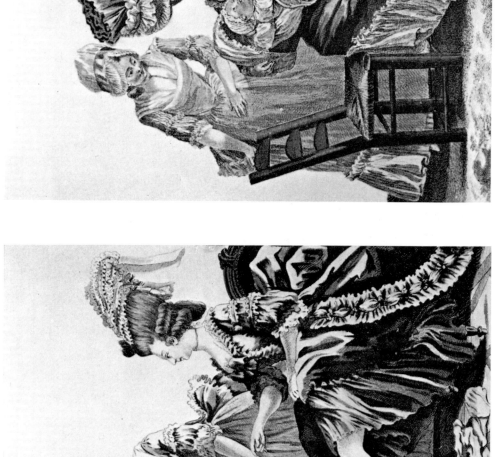

9　"Levite à Collet Peint". By Claude-Louis Desrais
From "La Gallerie des Modes," 1778

8　The Absent-minded Lady. By Claude-Louis Desrais
From "La Gallerie des Modes," 1778

teenth century, the female bosom was not considered to be the shameful object which it became in Victorian days, never to be mentioned and certainly not to be revealed in its entirety. So we have, in the *Gallerie des Modes*, delicious examples of how ladies were advised to make the most of their charms in this respect. There is a plate (1778), for instance (Fig. 7), which describes a *Mantelet à Coulisses*. I do not pretend to know what the correct interpretation of this may be nor, so far as my researches have gone, does anyone else; so I leave it to the inspection and analysis of the reader and give a free translation of its description:

"This mantle would seem, at first sight, to detract from the elegance of the dress which it covers; but the effect does not respond to the cause. This part of the costume, considered in relation to the rest of the adornment, may be compared with the shadows in a picture; anything that contributes to an illusion is very far from destroying it. The Summer Caraco is very short, leaving the bosom entirely free.

"So that it is not without reason that this Beauty has enveloped herself in this vast mantle with its turned-back ruching. With it she need have no fear that the most beautiful bosom will pass unnoticed.

"The costume proffered in this engraving exudes a note of voluptuousness from which it is hard to escape. And the model has been chosen from among those Beauties of whom Solomon said that they were quivers to hold many arrows."

Although the *Gallerie des Modes* does not strictly come into the subject-matter for this book, I have been unable to resist including two more of its delightful plates.

The first of these (Fig. 8), entitled *La Distraite*, or "The Absent-minded Lady", was designed by Leclère and engraved by Dupin; its description is as follows:

"This woman, having completely dressed herself, suddenly remembers that she has omitted to wash her feet. So she makes her maid bring her a basin of water. Her dress is of wine-grey tussore silk, the trimmings being of the same colour; the ribbon which floats down in front is of celestial-blue, knotted at intervals by little flowers. The ladies' maid wears a jacket made of pale Buras."

41

The preceding plate in the series shows a lady having her hair dressed, and the one at present under discussion adds the comment:

"The previous figure has presented us with the toilette of the head; this one offers us the toilette of the opposite end. 'Better late than never' is an old proverb of which our absent-minded lady is now taking full advantage. It is, however, much better not to be absent-minded and to do everything at its proper time."

My third plate from this series is called *Levite à Collet Peint*. Shall we say dressing-gown with a painted collar? (Fig. 9.) It was designed by Leclère and engraved by Patas, and is described as follows:

"Young woman having her child brought to her in a bassinet, so that she may suckle it during her outing. She is clad in a dressing-gown which has a hand-painted collar and is trimmed with muslin, as also are the cuffs of the garment.

"The elegant toilette of this loving mother may serve to show that strict morals are not incompatible with a taste for the most graceful and the latest fashions. The desire to make the most of the charms with which one has been gifted by nature is not always a crime; it is more often one of the results of a friendly disposition. Even when, in the good old days, the apple of discord made its appearance, goodness did not cease to be goodness merely because a prize for beauty was in dispute."

After the *Gallerie des Modes* came to an end in 1787, there was a gap in the production of really fine costume-plates until 1794, when Nicolaus Wilhelm von Heideloff appears upon the scene. Heideloff was born in Stuttgart in 1761, and was brought up to be an engraver. In the 1780s he migrated to Paris, where he lived by painting miniatures until the outbreak of the French Revolution dispersed his clientèle. We next hear of him in London, where he obtained employment with R. Ackermann, the famous bookseller and publisher of fine prints. This connection is significant in view of Ackermann's subsequent interest in fashion-plates; it is not known how long it lasted, but in April 1794, when Heideloff was thirty-three years of age, he struck out on his own and started issuing *The Gallery of Fashion*.

The Gallery of Fashion was nearer to the true fashion-plate than anything of its ambitious nature that had preceded it, though it was still meant to be more a record of existing modes than designs for the future. Indeed, in an advertisement announcing his forthcoming publication, Heideloff says that the dresses "are not imaginary but really existing ones", and he goes on to say that they are intended to be "a Repository of English National Dresses of Ladies".

This publication was issued in monthly parts, each part consisting of two aquatints, beautifully coloured by hand and enriched with gold, silver and other metallic tints. The yearly subscription was three guineas, and it lasted until March 1803, when it had completed exactly nine years of existence. Thus, with twenty-four plates issued each year (except in the second year, when the number was twenty-five), the total number of plates issued by Heideloff was 217. In addition to this, each yearly volume was supplied with a beautiful allegorical title-page, also in hand-coloured aquatint. And, of course, each plate was accompanied by a detailed description of the dresses which it depicted. Each plate showed either one, two or three figures, the total number shown being 362.

The groups of figures in *The Gallery of Fashion* are shown in a large number of different occupations, such as out driving in a berlin, playing and singing at the harpsichord or the harp, taking tea and strolling at the seaside with their children. They are provided with accessories, such as muffs, fans, telescopes, bonnets, books and parasols, to say nothing of dogs, watches, tippets, gloves and a vast variety of trinkets. The majority of the plates represent outdoor scenes.

The best of the Heideloff plates are, on the whole, better drawn than the plates in the *Gallerie des Modes*, but there is a sameness about the faces of the ladies and they lack the Gallic abandon of the *Gallerie*; on the other hand, owing to the incidence of the French Revolution, Heideloff had not such attractive material to work upon as had Desrais, Saint-Aubin and Watteau, with their rich laces and brocades.

We can arrive at a fairly accurate estimate of the circulation of *The Gallery of Fashion*, as in many of the volumes are given lists of subscribers. some of the booksellers, for instance, subscribed for several copies, one taking as many as thirty-six. So we find that the total number of copies subscribed for was 347 in Great Britain and sixty-seven abroad. It is therefore reasonable to say that the total issue was never more than 450 at any time of its career; the number of separate copies sold (at seven shillings and sixpence an issue) must have been very small.

From these lists of subscribers it appears that those for the first volume, in 1794, included the Princess Royal, the Princess Augusta, the Princess Elizabeth, the Duke of York and the Empress of Germany. It was not until volume IV began to appear in 1797 that we find the names of Her Majesty Queen Charlotte and Prince Edward (later Duke of Kent). There is a Mr. Victor Heideloff of Stuttgart who supported the family venture by taking eight copies; and Ackermann cautiously put himself down for four. In a later list comes the name of John Zoffany, renowned for his charming conversation pictures. Messrs. Colnaghi & Co. took eleven.

I think that the most intriguing subscriber is one who appears in the list at the end of volume III, among the "Foreign Subscribers" and is simply described as "A lady at Zelle". I wonder who she was. I picture her as an English lady of quality, young but no longer very young who, to escape from some scandal in which she had been involved at the English Court, had fled to Germany to live in obscurity and anonymity among the vineyards of the Moselle, quietly sipping her delicate Zeller Schlossberg or, even better, the delicious Schwarze Katz of a good year, while eagerly awaiting the monthly courier who would bring her *The Gallery of Fashion* to remind her of the vanished glories of the past.

The Gallery of Fashion, like the *Gallerie des Modes*, is a very difficult book to find in good condition and complete in every respect. There is a superb set in the Victoria and Albert Museum which, from a pencilled note at the end of the first volume, seems at one time to have changed hands for £260. The last complete copy that I have been able to trace was sold in New York for $1900. I believe that an intending purchaser would be lucky to acquire such a set today at twice that amount. Occasionally incomplete volumes and single plates can be found, but even these command high prices.

One of the puzzling aspects of *The Gallery of Fashion* is the way in which, after the first five volumes had appeared, the plates gradually

10　A Lady in Full Dress in
August 1770

From "The Lady's Magazine," 1770

11　Two Ladies at Ranelagh in the
Newest Dress

From "The Lady's Magazine," 1775

12　A Lady of Paris dressed in a
Taffety Polonee

*From "The New Lady's Magazine,"
1786*

13　Fashionable Full Dress of Paris

From "The Lady's Magazine," 1789

15 Summer Dresses in the Garden

From Heideloff's "Gallery of Fashion," September, 1794

14 Ladies in plain calico Morning Dresses

From Heideloff's "Gallery of Fashion," August, 1794

declined in design, execution and colour. It is obvious that something must have happened to Heideloff to cause this decline. In 1799 Heideloff was still under forty years of age, so it could not have been a case of senility. Neither is it likely that he suffered from any incurable disease, as after his publication came to an end he became once more connected with Ackermann and did not die until some forty years later.

Five plates from Heideloff's *Gallery of Fashion* are reproduced in this book (Figs. 14 to 17 and Plate I). The descriptions published with the plates are appended for their quaintness, in the Notes on the Illustrations.

Two other costume books that appeared at the beginning of the nineteenth century must be mentioned, to make the picture complete. The first of these is the *Almanach des Modes*, a yearly publication that appeared between 1814 and 1822. This almanac consisted largely of plates designed by Horace Vernet and Louis-Marie Lanté and engraved by Georges-Jacques Gatine and was designed more to show the oddities of fashion of the previous year than to be a fashion magazine. It contained the well-known series of "Merveilleuses" and "Incroyable" plates, which portrayed the extravaganzas of the ultra-fashionable youth of the period. An example of a Vernet-Gatine plate is given in Fig. 29.

The second book is *Le Bon Genre*, which was first published in 1817 and went through several editions. This is a record of English and French fashions since the beginning of the nineteenth century; the English fashions are more in the nature of caricatures, to show how badly English-women dress as compared with the Parisiennes.

In the next chapter I will deal in detail with the true fashion-plates and the periodicals in which they appeared. For purposes of convenience these have been divided into four periods, namely, 1770–1820, 1821–1842, 1843–1870 and 1871–1899. This division closely follows changes in the nature of the plates and magazines, in format and execution. Again for convenience, the history of some of the more important magazines has been traced from their beginning to the time when they ceased publication, even when this entails overlapping into the following period.

CHAPTER THREE

The First Period: 1770—1820

THE transition from the costume-plate to the true fashion-plate was, naturally, not a sudden one, and at the time when the publications described in the previous chapter were appearing, periodicals issuing true fashion-plates had already made their tentative bow.

Contrary to what might be expected, the first magazine, by many years, to issue fashion-plates with any regularity was not French but English, in the form of *The Lady's Magazine*, which started in 1770. The plates in this periodical, which was published monthly, were not, at first, issued coloured, though they were frequently coloured by their purchasers, especially dressmakers, to give a better idea of the appearance of the dresses. And it was probably this that led later to magazines giving their readers plates that were already coloured; certainly *The Ladies' Magazine* was issuing them so "embellished" by 1790. This magazine survived, in various forms and under different ownerships, until about 1837.

Fig. 10 shows the first fashion-plate from *The Lady's Magazine*, which appeared in August 1770. Apart from its title, "A Lady in Full Dress", no other description was given of it. Other eighteenth-century plates from this magazine, in 1775, 1786, 1789 and 1799 respectively, are shown in Figs. 11, 12, 13 and 15. These are exceptionally interesting as they show the transition from comparatively simple dress in 1775 to the extreme flamboyance of the period preceding the French Revolution, and the simplicity which followed it. Later plates from *The Lady's Magazine* in the early years of the nineteenth century are in Figs. 18 to 22, 37.

Towards the close of the eighteenth century quite a number of fashion

48

magazines began to make their appearance in England, France and Germany, the majority of them, oddly enough, coming from Germany. Most of these magazines were very short-lived, as will be seen from the hand-list at the end of the present chapter; few of them survived the turn of the century and many of them only existed for a few months.

The relative importance with which English and French fashions were regarded outside France at the end of the eighteenth century is indicated by the title of one German magazine which came out in 1793 and 1794. Translated, it was called *Magazine of the Latest Fashions from 'England, France and Germany*, England coming first.

Among the more important of these early magazines may be mentioned the *Cabinet des Modes* (1785–1789), continued as the *Journal de la Mode et du Goût* (1790–1793). This publication was issued in 143 parts; the complete series contains 356 plates, all of which, with the exception of some of the very early ones, were coloured by hand. The complete set is very rare indeed and commands a very high price when it comes on the market. A set was sold at auction in 1921 for about £300.

Other magazines which survived were the *Journal des Luxus und der Moden*, published in Weimar between 1786 and 1826, the *Journal des Dames et des Modes*, with very pretty plates headed "Costumes Parisiennes" and numbered consecutively between 1797 to 1839, and *The Ladies' Monthly Museum*, which started with very poor plates in 1798, but greatly improved between 1806 and 1829, and deteriorated again during the last three years of its existence, until it finally expired in 1832. The full title of the original production in 1897 is worth recording as a masterpiece of over-statement and the love of rodomontade titles. It reads as follows: *The Lady's Monthly Museum or Polite Repository of Amusement and Instruction: being an Assemblage of what can tend to Please the Fancy, Instruct the Mind or Exalt the Character of the British Fair.* Now what could be fairer than that?

There is also the Leipzig *Zeitung für die Elegante Welt* (1801–1850) and, of course, John Bell's monthly, *La Belle Assemblée*, one of the most important magazines of its time, and which contains some of the most delicate fashion-plates of all time. Some space must be devoted to the

Belle Assemblée, which occupies a very important position in the evolution of the fashion-plate. Its first number appeared in February 1806, about three years after *The Gallery of Fashion* came to an end.

John Bell was an enterprising character who left a very definite mark on the journalistic history of his time. He was a bookseller, a printer, a publisher, a type-founder and a newspaper proprietor. He was founder or part proprietor of many other periodicals, including *The Morning Post*, *The World* and *Bell's Weekly Messenger*. Born in 1745, he was therefore sixty-one when he entered on this new venture.

The full title of the magazine was *La Belle Assemblée, or Bell's Court and Fashionable Magazine addressed particularly to the Ladies*. Only a small part of the magazine was devoted to dress and fashion. The rest consisted of anecdotes of celebrities in the literary, musical and artistic world, and articles on needlework, painting and cooking; also poetry, politics and accounts of museums and exhibitions in London. It contained general observations on London and Paris fashions, and instructions on deportment and good manners and on the care of the complexion, the feet and the bosom. In fact, *La Belle Assemblée* really could be said to be a mine of useful information. Even the advertisements had a charm of their own as, apart from dressmaking and dress materials, they consisted of offers of cosmetics and beauty aids, such as rouges, false teeth, perfumery, patent corsets, powders, hair restorers and depilatories. One particularly attractive advertisement which went through a number of issues was a four-page advertisement for Urling's lace, consisting of steel engravings showing Urling's shop in the Strand and with small samples of the lace pasted on it to represent merchandise in the shop window. In addition, each number was "embellished" by a stipple portrait engraved by an expert engraver and two aquatint fashion-plates, details of which were given at length in the text.

At first, the fashion-plates issued with *La Belle Assemblée* were not coloured. But in October 1806, about eight months after its first publication, a gentleman calling himself John Browne Bell produced a rival monthly magazine which he named *Le Beau Monde*, the contents of which were so similar to those of John Bell's *La Belle Assemblée* that considerable confusion existed between the two magazines. As *Le Beau Monde* presented its readers with two well-executed hand-coloured fashion-plates, this was to John Bell's disadvantage; however, he rose to the occasion and after November 1806 *La Belle Assemblée* came out in two forms, one at half-a-crown with plain fashion-plates and one at three shillings and sixpence with the plates coloured by hand.

The plates of *La Belle Assemblée* fall naturally into five periods. In the first, from 1806 to 1809, the plates are very conventional and rather crudely coloured. It was not a very inspiring period; as one well-known French authority on fashion puts it, "between 1805 to 1814, fashion in Paris changed from week to week, with such delicate shades of change that it is almost impossible to distinguish between them".

The second period, from 1809 to 1820, is a great improvement on the first, in spite of the fact that under the Restoration women favoured white dresses in preference to coloured ones, which did not give much inspiration to the fashion-plate artist. In 1821 John Bell, then in his seventy-sixth year, disposed of *La Belle Assemblée*, and a new series of the magazine was started with a quite different type of plate; this is the beginning of the third period. The fourth period started in 1832, when the magazine appears to have changed hands again, and to have been edited by the Hon. Mrs. Norton, who was the original of George Meredith's *Diana of the Crossways*; and the title now became *The Court Magazine and Belle Assemblée*. For the next twenty-three years, that is to say, until 1854, the fashion-plates were very bad indeed; they do not deserve a place in any collection, being composed of inferior copies of plates from French magazines. They are also misleading, as they were often several months out of date. But in 1854 there was, if not a change of ownership, at any rate a change of editorship and policy, as *La Belle Assemblée* began to issue delightful plates by Héloïse Leloir (of whom more later), printed by Mariton in Paris, coloured there by hand and imported into England. The magazine continued for many years with these plates, until sometime in 1869, when it ceased to exist.*

* See *John Bell, 1745–1831,* by Stanley Morrison. University Press, Cambridge, 1930.

A representative collection of plates from *La Belle Assemblée* is reproduced here (Figs. 23 to 26, 39 to 41, 46, 49).

The next important contribution to the fashion-plate was when Rudolph Ackermann started the publication of his *Repository of Arts, Literature, Commerce, Manufactures, Fashions and Politics*. It has already been noted that Heideloff had been in the employ of Ackermann when he first came over to England, before he started *The Gallery of Fashion*; and it was no doubt the influence of this association that induced Ackermann to include fashion in his new venture. From its title it will be seen that *The Repository of Arts* was far from being an exclusively fashion magazine, but the fashion-plates were true fashion-plates, as they were intended to be a guide to ladies and their dressmakers.

The Repository of Arts was issued in monthly parts and contained, in addition to the fashion-plates, numerous plates showing, among other things, pictures, furniture and portraits. Two or more fashion-plates were included in each number, and were described in detail in the text. They were carefully designed, engraved in aquatint and coloured by hand; each plate contained one figure only, except in cases where children were included. The total number of fashion-plates in Ackermann's *Repository of Arts*, from the date of its inception until the time it ceased in 1829, was something like 450; a complete set is of great rarity and much to be prized.

Several of the earlier numbers of *The Repository of Arts* invited manufacturers of fancy goods to send in patterns of any new dress materials they made, adding that "if the requisites of Novelty, Fashion and Elegance are united, the quantity necessary for this magazine will be ordered". Three or four of the materials submitted were chosen, and small pieces of them were pasted on a setting described as "an allegorical woodcut". Descriptions of these materials were given on the page facing the woodcut, with the names and addresses of their manufacturers. The idea was no doubt inspired by the Urling's lace advertisements in *La Belle Assemblée*, but they form an interesting and attractive collection in themselves.

Unlike most of the early fashion magazines, which varied very much in quality as changes took place in their ownership and in the designers of their plates, *The Repository of Arts* maintained the high standard of excellence which it had set itself at the start, throughout its twenty-one years of existence. Indeed, in many ways it improved as it went on, many of the prettiest plates appearing during 1825–1829, its last five years. Examples of these plates are given in Figs. 27, 28, 30 to 36, 42, 44, 45; the later ones, between 1826 and 1829, have a charm and grace which is seldom found in the fashion-plates of the period.

One other magazine which deserves a mention and which started in this period is the first important Viennese fashion-paper, *Die Wiener Moden-Zeitung*, which flourished between 1816 and 1844, issuing about fifty-two plates a year during that time. They are, for the most part, charming plates, and are of great interest to the student of costume, as the Viennese women had their own fashions during the early years of the nineteenth century, just as the English ladies had theirs.

The fashion-plates of the first ten years of the nineteenth century were not very exciting. They were usually rather roughly drawn, contained one or two figures only, and had no backgrounds. Little attempt was made to give movement to the figures, which are there merely for the purpose of wearing the clothes. In addition to this, there was a rage for plain white garments with little or no ornamentation; and this, again, did not make the designing of coloured fashion-plates any easier.

After about 1811, however, colours began to return and more use was made of embroidery, particularly round the hems of the skirts, in which the patterns became almost formalised. This was, however, still in what Dr. Willett Cunnington calls "The Vertical Epoch", which lasted until 1820, when waists, which had for twenty years been worn just beneath the bosom, began to drop into their right position, and women began to have women's figures again. At the same time hats became increasingly more complicated.

And so we pass into the second period.

Fashion Periodicals : 1770—1820

Here follows a hand-list of the principal periodicals containing coloured fashion-plates which first appeared during the period covered by this chapter, namely, 1770 to 1820, together with the years during which they were published. In this list, as in all subsequent lists, the year of cessation of publication is sometimes only approximate, the year being the one after which no further issues appear to be known.

* * * * * *

$\dfrac{1770}{1837}$ The Lady's Magazine, *or* Entertaining Companion for the Fair Sex. (London)

$\dfrac{1782}{1789}$ Magazin für Frauenzimmer *and* Neues Magazin für Frauenzimmer. (Strasburg)

1784   Damen-Journal. (Berlin)

$\dfrac{1785}{1789}$ Cabinet des Modes, *renamed* Magasin des Modes Nouvelles, Françaises et Anglaises, *after the first year*. (Paris)

$\dfrac{1786}{1826}$ Journal des Luxus und der Moden. (Weimar)

$\dfrac{1786}{1794}$ Giornale delle Dame e delle Mode di Francia. (Italy)

$\dfrac{1787}{1790}$ Archiv Weiblicher Hauptkenntnisse. (Leipzig)

$\dfrac{1787}{?}$ Modefabriken und Gewerbes-Zeitung. (Prague)

$\dfrac{1788}{1795}$ Giornale delle Mode. (Florence)

16   Two Ladies at Breakfast in their Dressing-room

From Heideloff's "Gallery of Fashion," November, 1794

17   *From the "Lady's Monthly Museum," 1779*

18   Paris Dress

From "The Lady's Magazine," July, 1801

19   Paris Dress

From "The Lady's Magazine," March, 1801

20   Paris Dress
From "The Lady's Magazine,"
1803

21   Paris Dresses
From "The Lady's Magazine,"
May, 1804

22   London fashionable Mourning
Dresses
From "The Lady's Magazine," 1805

23   London Fashions, as worn in
December, 1806
From "La Belle Assemblée"

$\frac{1790}{1793}$	Journal de la Mode et du Goût, ou Amusemens du Salon et de la Toilette. (Paris). (*Sequel to* Le Magasin des Modes Nouvelles)
$\frac{1791}{1808}$	Journal für Fabrik, Manufaktur und Handlung. (Leipzig)
$\frac{1791}{1794}$	Kabinet van Mode en Smaak. (Haarlem, Holland)
$\frac{1793}{1794}$	Magazin der Neuesten Moden aus England, Frankreich und Teutschland (*sic*). (Stuttgart)
$\frac{1794}{1798}$	Allgemeines Europäisches Journal. (Brünn)
$\frac{1794}{1795}$	Berlinische Damen-Zeitung für Teutschland (*sic*). (Berlin)
1795	Moden-Gallerie. (Berlin)
$\frac{1795}{1799}$	Magazin für Freunde des Guten Geschmacks, der Bildenden und Mechanischen Künste, Manufakturen und Gewerbe. (Leipzig)
$\frac{1795}{1800}$	Berlinisches Archiv der Zeit und ihres Geschmacks. (Berlin)
$\frac{1797}{1817}$	Le Journal des Modes et Nouveautés. (Paris)
$\frac{1797}{1798}$	Figurini di Mode. (Florence)
$\frac{1797}{1839}$	Le Journal des Dames et des Modes ("Costumes Parisiens"). (Paris). German Edition 1799–1848 (Frankfurt). Belgian Edition 1818–?
$\frac{1798}{1806}$	Fashions of London and Paris. (London)

$\frac{1798}{1832}$	The Lady's Monthly Museum, or Polite Repository of Amusement and Instruction: being an Assemblage of what can Tend to please the Fancy, Instruct the Mind or Exalt the Character of the British Fair. Edited by a "Society of Ladies". (London)
$\frac{1798}{1810}$	London und Paris, eine Literarisch-Politische Zeitschrift. (Weimar)
$\frac{1799}{19-}$	Allgemeine Modenzeitung, ein Zeitschrift für die Gebildete Welt. (Leipzig)
$\frac{1799}{1800}$	Berlin, Eine Zeitschrift für Freunde der schönen Künste, des Geschmacks und der Moden. (Berlin)
$\frac{1799}{1801}$	Magazin des Neuesten Geschmacks in Kunst und Mode. (Leipzig)
$\frac{1799}{1806}$	La Correspondence des Dames, ou Journal des Modes. (Paris)
$\frac{1799}{1800}$	Musarion, ein Monatschrift für Damen. (Altona)
1799	Le Mois. (Paris)
$\frac{1801}{1859}$	Zeitung für die Elegante Welt. (Leipzig)
1801	Die Unsichtbaren. Eine Wochenschrift für Deutsche Frauen. (Frankfurt-am-Main)
$\frac{1802}{1806}$	Charis, ein Magazin für das Neueste in Kunst, Geschmack und Mode. (Leipzig)
1803	Le Miroir de la Mode. (London)
$\frac{1803}{1805}$	Pariser und Hamburger Damen- , Kunst- und Mode-Journal. (Hamburg and Altona)
$\frac{1804}{1828}$	Corriere delle Dame. (Milan)
1804	Eudora. Ein Tagblatt für Geschmack. (Nuremberg)

1804	The Elegances of Fashion and General Remembrancer of Taste and Manners, etc. (London)
1806 / 1868	La Belle Assemblée, or Bell's Court and Fashionable Magazine, addressed particularly to the Ladies. (London)
1806 / 1810	Le Beau Monde, or Literary and Fashionable Magazine. (London)
1807 / 1809	Record of Fashion and Court Elegance. (London)
1807 / 1810	Elegantia, of Tydschrift van Mode, Luxe en Smaak voor Dames. (Amsterdam)
1809 / 1811	Neues Journal für Fabriken, Manufakturen, Handlung, Kunst und Mode. (Leipzig)
1809 / 1828	The Repository of Arts, Literature, Commerce, Manufactures, Fashion and Politics. (London)
1809	Münchner Elegantes Sonntagsblatt für das Jahr 1809. (Munich)
1811 / 1815	Paris, Wien und London. Ein Fortgehendes Panorama dieser drei Hauptstädte. (Rudolstadt) (*Also called* London, Paris und Wien)
1814 / 1822	Almanach des Modes. (Paris)
1816 / 1844	Wiener Moden-Zeitung und Zeitschrift für Kunst, schöne Literatur und Theater. (Vienna)
1816 / 1848	Wiener Zeitschrift. (Vienna)
1818 / 1823	L'Observateur des Modes. (Paris)
1818 / 1819	The New British Ladies' Magazine. (London)
ca. 1820	L'Echo des Modes. (Paris)

CHAPTER FOUR

The Second Period: 1821—1842

THE fashion-plate designers of the 1820s were not slow to take advantage of the new developments in feminine fashions to elaborate their drawings.

The earlier costume-plates in the *Gallerie des Modes*, Heideloff's *Gallery of Fashion* and the *Almanach des Modes*, as well as many others, had all varied in size between large quarto and folio; they were not in any way restricted to size, as they were issued loose in parts, and any letter-press that may have accompanied them was incidental. But the early fashion magazines were mostly small octavo in size, and their plates had to conform to this. They became larger with *La Belle Assemblée* and *The Repository of Arts*, increasing to large octavo, about ten inches by six inches, and most of the other magazines followed suit for the whole of this second period. The plates still showed only one or two figures, but the designers began to put more grace and character and movement into them, particularly in the English magazines.

The 1820s were prolific years for the appearance of new magazines, and many of them were very long-lived. The *Petit Courrier des Dames*, which began the first year of its life as the *Nouveau Journal des Dames* in 1821, went on uninterruptedly until at least 1865. It was a weekly publication and included one or two fashion-plates with each issue.

The *Petit Courrier des Dames* was one of the most important of the French fashion magazines and contained, especially in its earlier and later stages, some of the best fashion-plates of the nineteenth century. The plates are not usually signed, but the styles of the best-known artists are easily recognisable and they can be identified without much difficulty. Until the 1840s it held its own with the other high-class magazines; it

60

24　Walking Fashions to be
worn in December, 1808
From "La Belle Assemblée"

25　Concert-room Full Dress
From "La Belle Assemblée",
November, 1809

26 Pelisse Walking Dress of
Autumnal Brown Sarcenet
From "La Belle Assemblée," 1810

27 Evening Dress
*From "Ackermann's Repository,"
October, 1811*

then had a slight relapse, but came to the fore again under the skilled draughtsmanship and engraving of Madame Florensa de Closmenil. Madame de Closmenil was reponsible for many fine fashion-plates in this paper, as well as in *La Mode*, the *Journal des Demoiselles* and *Le Bon Ton*; she had style and imagination and took trouble to place her figures in attractive and congenial surroundings, suitable to the clothes that the ladies were wearing. She usually signed her plates in full, including the "Madame", though sometimes she was content with "Florensa". Her plates of children's fashions are particularly happy. She really belongs to the next period, but she has been included here because her work is essentially bound up with the *Petit Courrier des Dames*.

Other artists who contributed largely to the success of this magazine were A. Pauquet, E. Préval, A. de Taverne, Laure Noël and Hervy. These artists all drew for a series of magazines, not necessarily connected, which had their editorial offices at No. 1 Boulevard des Italiens, which was later to become the Paris office of *The Queen*. Examples of plates from the *Petit Courrier des Dames* are given in Figs. 56 to 58, 60, 72, 73, 75, 92. There was a short-lived English version of this magazine called *The Ladies' Little Messenger* (Fig. 38).

An important new magazine with a very wide circulation started in London in 1824; this was *The World of Fashion*. The plates in this publication were slightly larger than the others, being square in shape and containing up to six figures. They never reached a very high standard of excellence, being almost invariably inferior copies of French plates, but they must be mentioned as they are the plates that are among the most frequently met with in England. The best plates the magazine produced were those engraved by W. Alais, in the early days of its existence; these are well and carefully designed (Fig. 43); even in the 1860s and 1870s, when nearly every English magazine imported its fashion-plates from France, *The World of Fashion* still issued its own plates, at that period mostly poor copies of plates by Héloïse Leloir.

In the same year, 1824, the first American fashion magazine appeared in Philadelphia. It was called *Graham's American Monthly Magazine of Literature, Art and Fashion*, and was modelled on *La Belle Assemblée*.

This publication also contained copies of English and French plates, engraved locally. A reproduction of a plate issued in 1841 is seen in Fig. 61. *Graham's Magazine* was published regularly until 1854; copies of it are not easy to find, and complete series are very rare; their value is a purely sentimental one; the actual fashions portrayed can often be traced to European magazines of anything up to a year before.

One of the most prolific sources of fashion-plates in England is *Townsend's Selection of Parisian Costumes* which, starting in 1823, consisted of sets of plates imported from France, accompanied by English descriptions. As a result, we have a remarkable record of French fashions from that date until 1888, when the issue came to an end. The plates in *Townsend's Selection* were chosen with the greatest care. Most of the earlier ones had originally appeared in *Le Journal des Dames et des Modes* and *Le Petit Courrier des Dames*. A little later, in 1826, Townsend economised for a short time by issuing badly executed plates bearing beneath them the words "Neeles, 352 Strand", but he soon returned to his imported plates, presumably finding that economy did not pay and that his sales were diminishing. It is fortunate for us that he did so, as, in consequence of his activities, the early plates from *Le Journal des Dames* and *Le Petit Courrier des Dames* are not particularly rare in England. When *Le Petit Courrier* came to an end, in 1865, Townsend's carried on from other sources.

Incidentally, of course, *La Belle Assemblée* and Ackermann's *Repository* were still flourishing in the 1820s and many of their more attractive plates were produced during these years.

In 1829 a Parisian magazine entitled *Le Follet Courrier des Salons* made its appearance. This contained by far the most stylish plates yet produced in France and marks the beginning of the gradual ousting of the English plates by the French. Some of them are really delightful, though it must be admitted that their charm owes a great deal to the absurdity of the fashions of the early 1830s, with their exaggerated sloping shoulders, leg-of-mutton sleeves in reverse and vast collars which looked more like the Chinese "kang" instrument of torture than portions of the raiment in which ladies took their ease. These collars did not survive for long, 1833 and 1834 at the most (see Figures 47 to 51). I suppose that the fashion dictators of the time held just as much sway as they do today, but I can only imagine that the worm turned. For other and later plates from *Le Follet*, see Figs. 52, 53, 59, 65, 81, 87, 88, 103 and Plate III. The earlier plates were not signed, but later, in the 1840s and 1850s, all the best fashion-plate designers worked for *Le Follet*, which was one of the longest-lived of all the fashion magazines and was still flourishing with hand-coloured plates in 1899. It was among the more important of the mid-century fashion magazines, and no collection of fashion-plates can be representative without it.

In 1829, too, Henri de Girardin founded his *La Mode*, which was to continue in circulation for twenty-five years. Shortly after the founding of this magazine, Girardin had the luck and the foresight to employ, in 1930, a young and brilliant draughtsman named Sulpice Guillaume Chevalier. In the previous year this young man had exhibited in the Paris Salon a water-colour drawing of a village in the Pyrenees called Gavarnie. The compiler of the exhibition catalogue confused the name of the artist with the title of the picture, which so amused the artist that he thenceforward adopted the name "Gavarny" as his *nom de pinceau*, the spelling being later changed to "Gavarni". Gavarni personified the spirit of Paris in his drawings and in his fashion-plates, in a way which no one had done before him. During the first two or three years of his connection with *La Mode*, he designed a weekly fashion-plate for it, but as time went on he contributed less and less and ceased to do so altogether in 1837. No fashion-plate designer before him had ever succeeded in making his models so feminine, or had been able to inspire them with so much vitality. A complete set of *La Mode* from 1830 to 1837 is very rare indeed. There are no volumes of this series in either the British Museum or the Victoria and Albert Museum, and even in print-shops only isolated examples turn up from time to time. The first plate reproduced here, Plate II, is in his most delightful vein and shows children at play. He was very fond of putting children into his fashion-plates, usually accompanied by adults. Two other plates by Gavarni in about 1837 are also given (Figs. 54 and 55).

Fashion-plates by Gavarni appeared in other periodicals during this decade and the next, but only spasmodically. Among the magazines to which he is known to have contributed were *Le Voleur* (which used the same plates as *La Mode*), *La Vogue*, *Le Journal des Gens du Monde* and *La Sylphide*. Many years later he contributed fashion-plates to *L'Abeille Impériale* which, as its name implies, flourished during the Second French Empire. Gavarni is, of course, not only known for his fashion-plates. His scenes of life in Paris and London are mordant pieces of satire on the underworlds of those cities, which led to his being dubbed "Le gavroche", i.e. the street arab. His best-known work is probably *Le Diable à Paris*. He visited London between 1847 and 1851 and exhibited at the Royal Academy in 1850. He died in Paris in 1866.

At about the time that Gavarni started drawing for *La Mode*, a second American magazine with coloured fashion-plates made its appearance in Philadelphia, in the form of *Godey's Ladies' Handbook*, a monthly publication which first came out in July 1830 and continued without a break until 1898. The earlier plates, like those of *Graham's Magazine*, were crude copies from French magazines, mostly from *Le Petit Courrier des Dames*; it was, indeed, more than probable that these had reached America through *Townsend's Fashions*; only one plate was issued each month. In the 1850s some of the actual metal plates were imported from France, notably from *Le Moniteur de la Mode*, presumably when these had become outdated and no longer represented the Paris fashions of the day; the captions on the plates were erased and fresh ones substituted, but the plates can easily be traced to their original sources; I traced one which had appeared in Paris eleven months before its appearance in America. It was a long and arduous voyage to America in those days, and a delay of months can quite be understood, particularly if the plates went out by cargo boat. Nowadays, Paris fashions are radioed to America and appear there almost before the mannequins have stopped displaying them!

The newly-engraved captions varied very much, and we find "Godey's Unrivalled Coloured Fashions", "Latest Fashions for Godey's Lady's Book", "The Latest Fashions, only to be found in Godey's Lady's Book" and "Godey's Coloured Fashions". *Godey's Ladies' Handbook* was one of the first outside Germany to abandon hand-coloured plates, and in

28   Walking Dress
From "Ackermann's Repository,"
September, 1812

29   (*Right*) Merveilleuse,
by Horace Vernet,
engraved by Gatine
From "Merveilleuses et
Incroyables," 1814

30   Pink and white striped percale half-dress
From "Ackermann's Repository," 1816

32   Morning Dress of embroidered clear lawn
From "Ackermann's Repository," 1819

31   Blue silk half-dress with a blond flounce
From "Ackermann's Repository," 1819

1890 issued some very crude colour prints which were a very retrograde step. It may be remembered that in *Gone With the Wind* one of the things that annoyed Scarlet O'Hara most about the American Civil War was that she could no longer get hold of Godey's fashions, Philadelphia being in the North. There is a complete set of *Godey's Ladies' Magazine* in the Library of the British Museum.

The 1830s were bad years for fashion-plates everywhere except in France where, though they were still very stylised, more effort seemed to be put into them. Three important magazines made their appearance in Paris during this decade: *Le Journal des Demoiselles* and *La Musée des Familles*, both in 1833 and *Le Bon Ton*, in 1834. *Le Journal des Demoiselles* continued well into the twentieth century, and the other two survived for at least forty years. They all three employed the very best of the fashion-plate designers, such as Pauquet, Portier, A. de Taverne, Laure Noël and others. Indeed, *Le Bon Ton* was one of the first magazines to employ Laure Noël, when she was nineteen years of age; she was still unmarried and signed her plates by her maiden name of Laure Colin (Fig. 66). She was one of the three famous Colin sisters, of whom I shall have more to say later. The others were Anaïs Toudouze and Héloïse Leloir. (For plates from these magazines see Figs. 64, 66, 71, 74, 76, 82, 83, 85, 86, 91, 118.)

The two most important English magazines to make their bow in the later part of this period were *The Ladies' Cabinet* (1832–1870) and a larger production, *The Ladies' Gazette of Fashions* (1842–1894). Both these magazines were published in London, both copied French plates and neither produced any plates worthy of the serious collector; they are, in fact, included here more as a warning than anything else, as to what to avoid. The plates of *The Ladies' Cabinet* are small octavo prints, badly drawn and coloured; those of *The Ladies' Gazette of Fashion* are large square plates divided into two by a horizontal line, the top, smaller part representing hats and accessories, the lower containing four or five figures clad in fairly recent fashions. In the meantime, *The Lady's Magazine* gave up the struggle of issuing its own plates and imported them from *Le Follet*; it was the first English magazine to import French plates, which were an immense improvement on anything being turned out in England at the time; the captions were slightly altered to include the words *The Lady's Magazine* somewhere on the plate, and sometimes a short description of the dress was also given in English. In these plates, though some of them were drawn by very good craftsmen, little attempt was made to give more than an almost diagrammatic view of prevailing fashions, very often only giving the front and back views of the same dress on the same plate.

But the romantic period was fast approaching, and this was to have a very definite influence on fashion and on the fashion-plate. Fashionable ladies at the end of the 1830s affected cynicism and eccentricity and aped the pursuits and manners of men. They were nicknamed "Lionnes", or Lionesses, after an improvised poem by Alfred de Musset in which he refers to the lady whom he calls elsewhere his "wild mad mistress with her Andalusian pallor" "ma maîtresse, ma lionne".

These so-called Lionnes were very provocative, with their swashbuckling airs, drinking deep, indulging in sword and pistol play, riding hard and even smoking cigars. They were ridiculed in caricature by Gavarni and other contemporary artists, and they gradually disappeared, their place being taken by two different categories of coquettes: the "tapageuses" or rowdies and the "mystérieuses". The characteristics of the first of these were their harum-scarum manners and highfalutin airs; the "mystérieuses" affected an aristocratic air of dignified reserve. And it is on this note that we enter upon our third fashion-plate period.

Fashion Periodicals: 1821—1842

Hand-list of the principal periodicals which first appeared with coloured fashion-plates during the period covered by this chapter, namely, 1821 to 1842, together with the years during which they were published.

* * * * * *

1821 —— 1829	L'Album, Journal des Arts, des Modes et des Théâtres. (Paris)
1821	Le Nouveau Journal des Dames ou Petit Courrier des Modes, des Théâtres, de la Littérature et des Arts. (Paris)
1822	Le Petit Modiste Français (*sic*). (Paris)
1822 —— 1865	Petit Courrier des Dames, ou Nouveau Journal des Modes, des Théâtres, de la Littérature at des Arts. (Paris)
1823	Fashion as it Flies, or the Ladies' Little Messenger of Parisian Fashions, Embellished with Engravings. (London)
1823	The Ladies Little Messenger. (London). *See previous item.*
1823 —— 1825	Magasin für Konst, Nyheter och Moder. (Stockholm)
1823 —— 1888	Townsend's Quarterly (*later* Monthly) Selection of Parisian Costumes. (London)
1824 —— 1891	The World of Fashion. (London)
1824 —— 1840	The Ladies' Pocket Magazine. (London)

$\frac{1825}{1827}$	Moskovskii Telegraph. (Moscow)
1826	Wiener Mode. (Vienna)
$\frac{1826}{1858}$	Graham's American Monthly Magazine of Literature, Art and Fashion. (Philadelphia)
$\frac{1827}{1842}$	The Court Magazine and Monthly Critic and Lady's Magazine; and Museum of the Belles-Lettres, Music, Fine Arts, Drama, Fashions, etc. (London)
1827	Le Bouquet. (Paris)
$\frac{1827}{1840}$	Neue Pariser Modeblätter. (Hamburg and Leipzig)
ca. 1828	La Réunion. Journal Littéraire et des Modes. (Paris)
$\frac{1828}{1829}$	L'Omnibus de la Toilette. (Paris)
$\frac{1828}{1846}$	Le Voleur, Gazette des Journaux Français et Étrangers. (Leipzig and Paris)
$\frac{1828}{1847}$	Der Spiegel für Kunst, Eleganz und Mode. (Ofen)
$\frac{1829}{1892}$	Le Follet, Courrier des Salons, Journal des Modes. (Paris)
$\frac{1829}{1854}$	La Mode, Revue des Modes, Galerie des Moeurs, Album des Salons. (Paris)
ca. 1829	Pariser Modenzeitung für Deutsche Frauen.
ca. 1829	La Vogue. (Paris)
1830	Le Lys, Chronique de la Cour. Modes. Théâtres, Litterature. (Paris)
$\frac{1830}{1898}$	Godey's Ladies' Book. (Philadelphia)

33   Evening Dress of gossamer satin
From "Ackermann's Repository," 1819

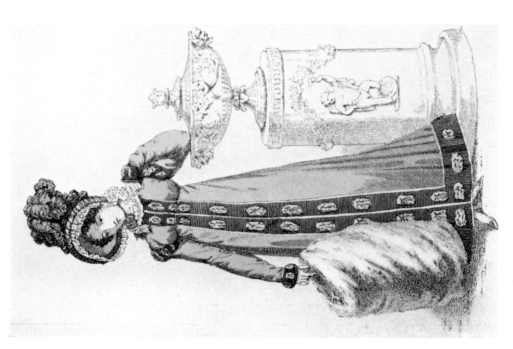

35   Evening Dress
From "Ackermann's Repository," June, 1820

34   Walking Dress of grey merino
From "Ackermann's Repository," 1819

36 Green Promenade Pelisse
    of gros de Naples

From "Ackermann's Repository,"
1821

37 Carriage Dress

From "The Lady's Magazine," 1823

38   High Dress of *gros de Tours* silk. Front and back views
From "The Ladies' Little Messenger," 1823

39   Summer Recess Costume
From "La Belle Assemblée,"
September, 1825

40   Carriage Costume
From "La Belle Assemblée,"
April, 1826

41   Indoors Costume
From "La Belle Assemblée," October, 1826

42   Ball Dress
From "Ackermann's Repository,"
July, 1827

43   Fashionable Head-dresses and Seaside Riding Dresses
From "The World of Fashion," July, 1828

44   Dinner Dress
From "Ackermann's Repository,"
February, 1829

45   Opera Dress
From "Ackermann's Reposi-
tory," March, 1829

46   Archery Dresses
From "La Belle Assemblée,"
September, 1831

47   *Crêpe de Chine* Dress
From "Le Follet Courrier des Salons,"
1831

48 Muslin Dress, with an embroidered *gros de Naples* apron. The child's dress is of jaconet

From "Le Follet Courrier des Salons," August, 1832

49 Walking Dress.
Front and back views
From "Le Follet Courrier des Salons,"
1833

$\frac{1830}{1831}$	Le Mercure des Salons, Revue Française et Étrangère. (Paris)
$\frac{1831}{1835}$	The Royal Ladies' Magazine and Archives of the Court of St. James's. (London)
$\frac{1832}{1833}$	Der Conversations-Freund. (Hanau)
$\frac{1832}{1836}$	Schnellpost für Moden und Literatur. (Leipzig)
$\frac{1832}{1834}$	Allgemeine Weltchronik unserer Zeit. (Frankfurt)
$\frac{1832}{1849}$	Berliner Modenspiegel In- und Ausländische Originale. Ein Zeitschrift für die Elegante Welt. (Berlin)
$\frac{1832}{1863}$	Le Journal des Jeunes Personnes. (Paris)
$\frac{1832}{1870}$	The Ladies' Cabinet of Fashions. (London)
$\frac{1833}{1872}$	Le Beau Monde. (*Revived*) (Paris and London)
$\frac{1833}{19—}$	Le Journal des Demoiselles. (Paris)
$\frac{1833}{1891}$	La Musée des Familles ("Modes Vraies"). (Paris and Brussels)
$\frac{1833}{1834}$	La Revue des Modes de Paris. (Paris)
$\frac{1834}{1874}$	Le Bon Ton. Journal des Modes. (Paris)
$\frac{1834}{1840}$	Le Messager des Salons. (Paris)

$\frac{1834}{1854}$	Psyche (La Toilette de Psyche), Journal de Modes, Sciences, Littérature et Beaux-Arts. (Paris)
1834	Journal des Gens du Monde. (Paris)
$\frac{1835}{1836}$	Omnibus, Journal Mensuel de la Littérature, des Anecdotes, des Faits Politiques, des Théâtres, de la Musique et des Modes. (The Hague)
ca. 1835	Le Protée. (Paris)
$\frac{1835}{1837}$	La Gazette des Salons, Journal des Modes, et de la Musique, Artistique, Littéraire et Théâtral. (Paris)
$\frac{1835}{1843}$	Le Miroir des Dames. (Paris)
$\frac{1835}{1885}$	Europa, Chronik der Gebildeten Welt. (Leipzig, Stuttgart and Karlsruhe)
ca. 1835	La Lanterne. (Paris)
$\frac{1836}{1837}$	Museum der Eleganten Welt. (Munich)
$\frac{1836}{1840}$	Paris Élégant, Journal des Modes, Chronique des Salons, des Théâtres, de la Littérature et des Arts. (Paris)
$\frac{1836}{1854}$	Longchamps et Paris Élégant. (Paris)
$\frac{1836}{1854}$	Le Caprice, Journal de la Lingerie, Revue des Modes, contenant des Articles sur le Costume, le Musique et la Littérature. (Paris)
$\frac{1837}{1843}$	Eilpost für Moden, Neue Zeitschrift für Kunst und Moden. (Leipzig)
$\frac{1837}{1838}$	L'Aspic, Moniteur Générale des Modes. (Paris)

$\dfrac{1839}{1854}$ La Sylphide. (Paris)

$\dfrac{1839}{1840}$ Der Telegraph von Berlin. (Berlin)

$\dfrac{1839}{1848}$ Pariser Moden-Journal (and Neuestes ditto), eine Uebersetzung der Neuesten Pariser Moden-Berichte, nebst Angabe des Schnitts. (Ulm)

$\dfrac{1840}{1848}$ Dziennik Domowy (Journal for the House). (Posen)

$\dfrac{1840}{1844}$ Le Journal des Femmes. (Paris)

$\dfrac{1840}{1844}$ L'Oriflamme des Modes. (Paris)

$\dfrac{1840}{1942}$ La Renaissance. (Paris)

$\dfrac{ca.\ 1840}{1844}$ Le Cabinet de Lecture. (Paris)

ca. 1840   Le Propagateur des Modes. (Paris)

$\dfrac{1841}{1842}$ L'Avenir. (Paris)

$\dfrac{1841}{1842}$ Le Monde Dramatique. (Paris)

ca. 1841   Les Coulisses. (Paris)

$\dfrac{1841}{1862}$ El Correo del Ultramar (Madrid).

$\dfrac{1842}{1871}$ Die Elegante. (Vienna)

$\dfrac{1842}{1874}$ Jahreszeiten, Hamburger Neue Mode-Zeitung. (Hamburg)

$\dfrac{1842}{1885}$ La Moda Elegante Illustrada, Periódico de las Familias. (Madrid)

$\dfrac{1842}{1894}$ The Ladies' Gazette of Fashion. (London)

*　*　*　*　*　*

The following are the periodicals from the previous list which overlap into the present period. The year of their first publication is given in brackets.

> The Lady's Magazine (1770).
> Journal des Luxus und der Moden (1786)
> Le Journal des Dames et des Modes (1797)
> The Lady's Monthly Museum (1798)
> Allgemeine Moden-Zeitung (1799)
> Zeitung für die Elegante Welt (1801)
> Corriere delle Dame (1804)
> La Belle Assemblée (1806)
> The Repository of Arts (1809)
> Almanach des Modes (1814)
> Wiener Moden-Zeitung (1816)
> L'Observateur des Modes (1818)

50   White muslin dress
From "Le Follet Courrier des Salons," 1834

51   Organdie dress embroidered with
satin-stitch
From "Le Follet Courrier des Salons," 1834

52   Plaid silk dress
From "Le Follet Courrier des Salons," 1835

53   A dress embellished with lattice-net
*From "Le Follet Courrier des Salons,"
March, 1836*

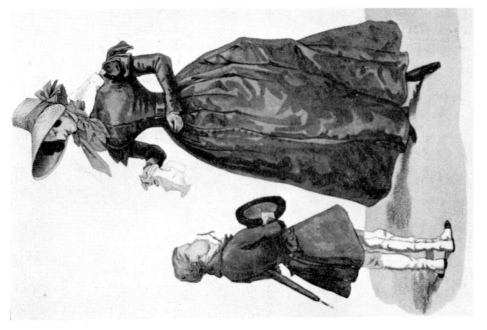

55   Promenade Dress. By Gavarni
From "La Mode," c. 1837

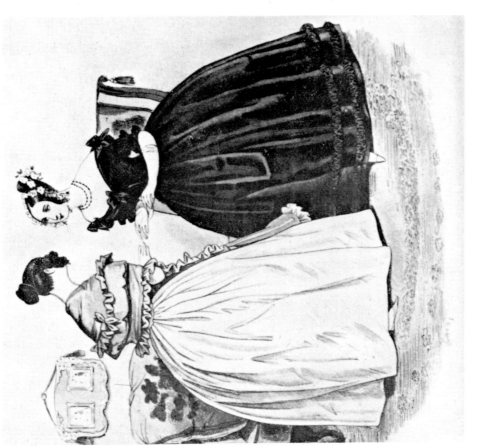

54   A dress of satin brocade and a velvet dress decorated with
black tulle ribands. Designed by Gavarni
From "La Mode," February, 1837

56   Satin corset by Monsieur Josselin. Signed Barreau
From "Le Petit Courrier des Dames," July, 1837

57   Wedding Dress of
renaissance lace

*From "Le Petit Courrier des
Dames," November, 1838*

58   Wedding Dress and Longchamps Toilette

*From "Le Petit Courrier des
Dames," 1839*

59   Morning Dress of striped Pekin and tulle Wedding Dress
From " Le Follet Courrier des Salons," 1840

60   Riding Habit
From " Le Petit Courrier des Dames," September, 1841

61 Fashions for April 1841

From "Graham's Magazine," Philadelphia

63 Country Dresses. Engraved by Réville after Jules David
From " Le Moniteur de la Mode," 1844

62 Morning and Afternoon Dresses. Engraved by Gervais
after Jules David
From " Le Moniteur de la Mode," 1843

64   Evening Dresses. By Madame Florensa de Closménil

From "Le Bon Ton," 1845

CHAPTER FIVE

The Third Period : 1843—1870

WE now enter upon what, in my opinion, is the Golden Age of the fashion-plate. In this I am in slight disagreement with Doris Langley Moore and James Laver, because they are concerned mainly with the designs of the costumes, whereas I am more interested in the execution of the plates. And I feel that fashion-plates of this period reached their highest level.

In 1843 two Paris publications, the *Moniteur de la Mode* and *Les Modes Parisiennes*, brought an entirely new atmosphere into the fashion-plate. Instead of presenting the fashions in stilted and stylised form to be followed as best might be, they began to make their pictures live and, as it were, to make "conversation pieces" of them. *Les Modes Parisiennes* was the earlier of the two magazines by a few months, starting at the beginning of March, though they were both probably conceived at the same time and, of the two, the *Moniteur de la Mode* was the most artistic.

The artist mainly responsible for the *Moniteur de la Mode* was Jules David, a painter and lithographer who was born in 1808 and had first exhibited in the Paris Salon of 1834. He was well known in his day as a book illustrator. There is a charming children's edition of *Don Quixote* in Spanish illustrated by him and published in Paris in 1888, when he was eighty years of age. Though little is known of Jules David's life, to everyone who has studied or collected fashion-plates his name conjures up a long series of some of the most charming plates of the Victorian era. He introduced elaborate backgrounds into his drawings, a practice which was followed by all his successors. One finds interiors which are in themselves valuable documentation of the décor and falderals of the period. The

93

drawing-roon, the dining-room, the boudoir, the music room, were all represented, while ladies in summer dresses strolled about in ornamental, bepergola-ed gardens, or displayed their toilettes on the lawns of the Longchamps or Auteuil racecourses, quite oblivious to the efforts of the striving horses in the offing. But the ladies themselves were not just dummies on which clothes were hung, but seemed to take an interest in life and to be trying to live it well.

All Jules David's fashion-plates were designed for the *Moniteur de la Mode*. But they subsequently appeared in many other French magazines, as well as in German, English, Spanish and even American publications such as the *Monitor of Fashion*, published in New York in 1853–1854. He remained faithful to the *Moniteur* until the day of his death, which occurred in 1892, two months after his last fashion-plate was issued and nearly fifty years since his first plate had appeared in that magazine. Several examples of his work are reproduced here (Figs. 62, 63, 68, 84, 97, 100, 102, 106). His style is always easily recognisable, but his plates have the additional advantage that they were always signed, so that no mistake is possible. He produced about 2600 plates for the *Moniteur de la Mode*; a complete collection of these would be a perfect history of the fashions of those fifty years. After David's death his place in the *Moniteur* was taken by G. Gonin and others (Figs. 121, 123); the magazine itself was still flourishing in the early years of the present century.

We next come to *Les Modes Parisiennes* (1843–1875), with its sub-title *Le Keepsake des Dames* which, with the *Moniteur de la Mode*, were by far the most important magazines started in the 1840s. The chief artist of *Les Modes Parisiennes* was François-Claudins Compte-Calix (1813–1880); he was an artist of some repute who exhibited water-colours at the Paris Salon for many years; he also illustrated a number of books on historical costume. Commenting on his work, Bénézit says: "Pretty and somewhat affected and sometimes a little weak in drawing, but graceful in treatment and pleasing in colour, his pictures reflect the poetic and sentimental aspirations of his time."

Whenever *Les Modes Parisiennes* is referred to in books dealing with costume, the date of its first issue is always given as January 1844. The

94

magazine started in March 1843, when it was the size of a modern illustrated weekly paper and contained fashion-plates of the same size; it was,
in fact, the largest paper of its kind that had hitherto appeared. However,
the size of the paper was reduced to quarto in January 1844. The reason
for the reduction is given in an editorial note which ran as follows: "The
condition in which our large paper has been reaching our subscribers,
after being mishandled by the postal service, has compelled us to reduce
Les Modes Parisiennes to a size that can travel without becoming creased."
Sets of the magazine almost invariably start with the January 1844 number; even the title-page, to be used if the numbers were to be bound
together, bore the words "Première Année". If any further proof were
wanted of the date of the first issue, the fashion-plates were numbered
consecutively from the beginning, and the plates for the year 1844 were
numbered from 45 to 96. For plates from this paper, see Figs. 69, 70, 77,
78, 80, 89, 90, 93, 95, and Plate IV.

The fashion-plates in the *Petit Courrier des Dames* and in the *Journal
des Demoiselles* in the 1850s were very refreshing in their *naïveté*. Consider
the ladies taking their ease on a balcony by the seaside after luncheon
(Fig. 73), seated on a swing (Fig. 74) or playing the rather bold game of
blind-man's-buff in the garden, with an ornamental fountain and a statue
of Diana in the background (Fig. 75).

Le Follet also had some delightful plates during this period. It
specialised in scenes at the opera (Fig. 81) and at soirées (Figs. 65, 88).
Most of the best drawings in this magazine after 1844 were from the hand
of Anaïs Toudouze.

Other noteworthy French fashion papers that originated in this period
and survived for a considerable number of years were the *Magasin des
Demoiselles* (1844–1893), *La Mode Artistique* (1860–19—) (Fig. 124)
and *La Mode Illustrée* (1860–19—) (Fig. 94). *La Mode Illustrée* was
one of the most important publications of its kind to appear in the second
half of the nineteenth century. It was one of the first magazines to make a
regular feature of ladies' underclothing, though even then the illustrations
never showed them on the person, but merely discreetly folded to show
details of lace and embroidery. Other magazines had, it is true, occasionally

95

come out with pictures of corsets, but they were not considered to be so esoteric as underclothing, as it was not so very long since the corset was a visible part of a lady's gown *La Mode Illustrée* was published every Sunday and had a circulation of about 20,000 copies.

In the same period *Die Modenwelt* (1860–19—) began to appear in Berlin. This probably had a wider circulation than any other fashion magazine in the nineteenth century. *Die Modenwelt* was published in fourteen different languages, under different titles; the English version was called *The Season* (Fig. 122). A full list of all its editions will be found in the hand-list of magazines at the end of this chapter; the plates were the same for all the editions, except for the captions, which were in the language of the country of issue.

Until this period, English fashion magazines, with the exception of *The Lady's Magazine*, gave their readers fashion-plates engraved in England. Indeed, the only French plates to be found, apart from imported French magazines, were those in *The Lady's Magazine* and *Townsend's Selection*. But with the introduction of the new style of French fashion-plate in 1843, most of the English magazines appear to have slowly given up the unequal fight and began to give their gentle readers what they really wanted, namely, the genuine French plates.

We now come to two of the most important of all the English fashion magazines, namely, *The Englishwoman's Domestic Magazine* and *The Queen*, both of which were founded by Samuel Beeton, the husband of the famous Mrs. Beeton who wrote the world-renowned cookery book and *The Book of Household Management*.

The Englishwoman's Domestic Magazine first appeared in 1852 and was, at first, only incidentally a fashion magazine, and published no coloured fashion-plates, though a few rather uninspiring black and white drawings purporting to portray the latest French fashions appeared in it from time to time. However, in 1860 Samuel Beeton had an inspiration and decided to follow the example of *La Belle Assemblée* and other English fashion papers and to import coloured fashion-plates from Paris for his magazine. In doing this he was either very intelligent or very well advised, because the plates which he selected were those of Jules David, from the *Moniteur*

66   Afternoon Dresses. Engraved by Boilly after Laure Colin
From "Le Bon Ton," 1847

65   Evening Dresses
From "Le Follet Courrier des Salons," 1846

67　Afternoon Dresses. By Anaïs Toudouze
From "Le Journal des Jeunes Filles," 1848

Children Skipping. By Gavarni
From "La Mode," 1830

PLATE II

Children's Fashions

From "Le Follet, Courrier des Salons," 1837

PLATE III

de la Mode, and no better selection could have been made. And for over twenty-five years one of these appeared every month in *The English-woman's Domestic Magazine*, until in 1877 it was incorporated in a publication bearing the singularly unromatic title of *The Milliner, Dressmaker and Warehouseman's Gazette*, which continued to issue the Jules David plates until it, too, came to an end in 1881.

Quite apart from its fashion-plates, the reports of fashions and foibles in *The Englishwoman's Domestic Magazine* make the most entertaining reading. For instance, in a detailed description of a bride's trousseau in 1861, seventeen varieties of petticoats are listed and eight sorts of drawers and pantalettes.

The Queen appeared nine years after *The Englishwoman's Domestic Magazine*, in 1861. It has the distinction of being the oldest fashion magazine in the world still to be published today. Its full title, as given in its first issue, was *The Queen, the Ladies' Newspaper*.

The Queen was a new departure in English fashion magazines as, although it started as a weekly publication, its format was more that of a daily newspaper, and it was registered, not as a magazine, but as a newspaper. During the first year of its existence *The Queen* contained very little information about fashion or dress, being more concerned, as was Samuel Beeton himself, with social activities and occupations, as well as literature and amusements which might be considered to be suitable and, within reason, of special interest to ladies.

However, Samuel Beeton does not seem to have made much of a success of his new venture as in the following year, 1862, he sold *The Queen* to William Edward Cox, who was already the proprietor of *The Field*. Two more incompatible papers could hardly be imagined!

Cox completely reorganised *The Queen* and, while retaining all the social side of the paper, introduced a stong dress and fashion element into it. A few uncoloured fashion-plates appeared in the paper in 1861, but Cox now went to Paris and made arrangements to have fashion-plates sent over to him regularly for his paper. He, again, was lucky or discriminating in his choice, for he chose the plates that were being issued with the *Petit Courrier des Dames*, most of which were being drawn, at that time, by A. Pauquet, an admirable fashion-plate artist who was working for both that paper and the *Journal des Demoiselles*. Indeed, the Paris address of *The Queen* was given as No. 1 Boulevard des Italiens, which was also the address of the editorial offices of the *Petit Courrier des Dames*. A little later plates began to appear by E. Préval, one of the artists of the *Journal des Demoiselles*. All these early plates were much smaller than the magazine itself, the reason, of course, being that the French magazines for which they were originally drawn were themselves so much smaller than *The Queen*.

However, in the later 1860s the plates grew to the size of the paper itself and on these, all of which were still imported from Paris, we find many of the most well-known and admired names in the art—A. Chaillot, G. Gonin, L. Leloup and, later, Isabelle Toudouze, a lady with whom I am sure, had I been a little older at the time, I would have fallen in love, for her name as well as for her art (Figs. 107, 109).

Each of the plates in *The Queen* contained two adult figures and often a child as well, though occasionally plates were issued which contained nothing but children's clothes, and these might contain half-a-dozen figures. But in 1885 a new system was adopted, which was to select ten or twelve large French fashion-plates and to have them reduced to one large plate. These were not very artistic or successful, though they appear to have persisted, with occasional alternation of French plates, until 1888, when an entirely new series of admirable plates took their place. These new plates were engraved by A. Sandoz and, from the collector's point of view, are some of the most fascinating fashion-plates, and certainly the most artistic, produced in the last quarter of the nineteenth century. That they were English is quite certain, as the background of the plates were essentially English and, in any case, these plates never appeared in any magazine outside England.

Sandoz did not copy the plates from the French papers, which had almost a monopoly of fashion-plates at the time, but he was undoubtedly inspired by them. When I say "he", I am making a guess, as no information is available about this artist, not even about his or her sex, but the plates were certainly the best produced in England since the 1820s. They are all dated and are described as "Latest Parisian Fashions". One of them was given as a supplement with the first number of *The Queen* issued each month (Figs. 115, 117, 119, 125, 126, 127).

Sandoz contributed his (or her) plates to *The Queen* from 1888 until 1898, when *The Queen* abandoned the hand-coloured plate for the colour-printed plate, which was a sadly retrograde step. It is, however, a great deal in favour of *The Queen* that it was the last English fashion magazine to retain the hand-coloured plate. I am much indebted to the present editor of *The Queen* for allowing me to browse among the extremely interesting archives of the paper which, I hope, will still be in a robust state of health in six years' time, when it will have attained its centenary, an achievement which no other English or French fashion magazine has ever succeeded in effecting.

We now come to the end of the Third Period, which brings us up to the Franco-Prussian War of 1870, which was another turning-point in the world of fashion; for, just as the Napoleonic Wars had completely changed women's clothes in the early years of the century, so the Franco-Prussian War entirely changed them also, but in a different way. For whereas the Napoleonic Wars had simplified women's clothes to a point at which ladies could almost appear naked in public, the 1870 war brought a fantastic elaboration in feminine costume, millinery and hair. A glance at the fashion plates of the 1870s will bear me out in this.

There were several American fashion magazines circulating during this period, but most of them did not contain coloured plates. Among these were *Peterson's Magazine*, *The Chicago Magazine of Fashion*, *Music and Home Reading*, and *Frank Leslie's Ladies' Gazette of Fashion* (New York 1854–1871), which occasionally issued coloured French plates (Fig. 99).

The dominant position attained by the French fashion-plate designers in the mid-nineteenth century is well illustrated by the difficulties in which fashion magazines found themselves at the end of 1870, soon after the outbreak of the Franco-Prussian War, when Paris was besieged and held practically no communication with the outside world. The Prussians naturally cut the telegraph lines; there was no radio; there were no aeroplanes. A few balloons went out, carrying news and urgent correspondence, but there was no knowing when and where they would come down;

many fell into the hands of the Prussians and some even came to grief in the English Channel. There was certainly no way in which fashion-plates could be sent out.

Miraculously, most of the Paris fashion papers carried on; but for the rest of Europe there was suddenly a dead blank in Paris fashions. Even German magazines complained that the war, however much it might add glamour to the Prussian man, did nothing to improve the dowdiness of the Prussian woman.

The siege of Paris began on September 20th, 1870, and ended with its capitulation on January 30th, 1871; and during this time and for some months afterwards the fashion magazines of other countries had to do the best they could. Isolated copies of French fashion papers occasionally filtered through, and these were copied, usually rather roughly, and printed in Holland, Belgium and England for distribution. Descriptions of the latest fashions were also contained in the newspapers, microscopically printed on flimsy paper, which were sent out by balloon to tell people what was happening in Paris; and plates were designed from these descriptions. Collecting these wartime fashion-plates makes an interesting study, but they are not very easy to get, as they were, for the most part, so poorly executed that they were not preserved.

As an example of the shifts to which fashion papers were put during the Franco-Prussian War, this is what happened to *The Queen*. The editor of *The Queen* was apparently caught unawares. The first September 1870 issue had contained the usual large plate by Isabelle Toudouze; it was one of her happiest efforts and showed a bride in her wedding dress admiring herself in a mirror and handing a sprig of orange-blossom to another version of herself in evening toilette, both dresses being trimmed with orange-blossom; this plate appeared in several papers at the time, including *Le Follet* and *Le Monde Élégant* (Fig. 96).

However, the first issue for October contained, instead of the usual fashion-plate, the following announcement:

"We regret to inform our subscribers that owing to the disturbed state of affairs in Paris, and the interruption of external communica-

69 Afternoon Dresses. By François-Claudins
Compte-Calix

From "Les Modes Parisiennes," 1850

68 Afternoon and Evening Dresses. Engraved by Réville
after Jules David

From "Le Moniteur de la Mode," September, 1849

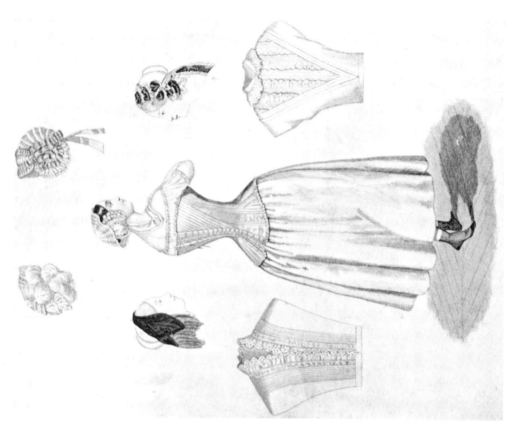

71   Corset and Lingerie

From " Le Bon Ton," 1850

70   Evening Dresses. By Compte-Calix

From " Les Modes Parisiennes," 1850

tions, the coloured fashion-plate which it has been our custom to publish with *The Queen* on the first Saturday of each month has not arrived in time for this issue. We have had advices from the besieged city that they are awaiting the re-establishment of facilities of transport. Although our subscribers will understand that the delay is thoroughly unavoidable, we beg to express our sorrow for any probable inconvenience caused thereby."

Nothing more happened until December 10th, when an uncoloured plate, poorly lithographed by A. Goater of Nottingham, appeared. This plate showed four dresses and was accompanied by the following notice:

"The accompanying fashions have been procured from Lyons at great trouble and cost. Our subscribers may avail themselves of them with perfect confidence in their genuineness and novelty. Notwithstanding the present interregnum, Paris must always remain the source of fashions."

The experiment was repeated in January, February and March. But in April the French plates were resumed in *The Queen*, the first one being promenade and outdoor toilettes by Anaïs Toudouze, Isabelle's mother.

Two other English magazines which started in this period, and of which careful note must be taken, were *The Lady's Treasury* (1858–1895) and *The Young Englishwoman*, which started in 1865 and in 1877 changed its name to *Sylvia's Home Journal*, under which title it survived until 1895. Both these magazines published good French plates, except for a short period in the middle 1880s, when *The Lady's Treasury* for some reason took to issuing very badly executed plates made in England.

When the war was over and things in Paris began to settle down again, fashion entered, as I have indicated, upon a new phase, a phase of pleats, ribbons, lace and bonnets perched on the top of far more hair than one woman in a thousand could ever have grown herself. Hair, indeed, was such a scarce commodity that many a poor girl with really luxuriant tresses got herself a comfortable dowry by selling it.

And so we pass to the fourth and last period, towards the end of which the hand-coloured fashion-plate died a lingering death, greatly mourned by all but the fashion magazines themselves.

Fashion Periodicals : 1843—1870

Hand-list of the principal periodicals with coloured fashion-plates which first appeared during the period covered by this chapter, namely, 1843 to 1870, together with the years during which they were published.

*   *   *   *   *   *

1843	La Péri. (Paris)
1843	Le Petit Messager des Modes. (Paris)
$\frac{1843}{19—}$	Le Moniteur de la Mode. (Paris)
$\frac{1843}{1875}$	Les Modes Parisiennes. (Paris)
$\frac{1844}{1854}$	Journal für die Moderne Stickerei, Mode und Weibliche Handarbeiten. (Weimar)
ca. 1844	La Gazette des Salons. (Paris)
1844	La Pie Voleuse. (Paris)
$\frac{1844}{1851}$	Der Putz-Tisch, Zeitung für Damenschneider, Modehandlungen, Stickerinnen. (Weimar)
$\frac{1844}{1893}$	Le Magasin des Demoiselles. (Paris)
$\frac{1845}{1848}$	La Mode des Demoiselles. (Paris)
$\frac{1845}{1853}$	Le Favori des Dames. (Paris)
$\frac{1845}{1851}$	Le Journal des Demoiselles. (Brussels)

$\frac{1846}{19-}$	Le Follet (English version). (Paris)
$\frac{1846}{1851}$	Illustrirtes Magazin begleitet von der Schnellpost für Moden. (Leipzig)
$\frac{1846}{19-}$	The (Minister's) Gazette of Fashions and Cutting-Room Companion. (London)
$\frac{1847}{1863}$	Le Conseiller des Dames et des Demoiselles, Journal d'Économie Domestique et de Travaux à l'Aiguille. (Paris)
$\frac{1848}{1871}$	Der Follet (German version). (Aachen)
$\frac{1848}{1861}$	Pariser Damenkleider Magazin. (Stuttgart)
1849	Journal des Jeunes Filles. (Paris)
$\frac{1849}{1857}$	Le Journal des Dames. (Paris)
$\frac{1849}{1863}$	Damen-Zeitschrift Iris Pariser Moden-, Muster- und Kleider-Magazin. (Gratz)
$\frac{1850}{1870}$	The Ladies' Companion at Home and Abroad. (London)
$\frac{1850}{1872}$	Cendrillon, ou la Fée des Foyers, Journal des Petites Demoiselles. Revue Encyclopédique de Tous les Travaux de Dames. (Paris)
1850	Le Glaneur. Gazette des Journaux Français. (Leipzig)
$\frac{1851}{1852}$	Il Folletto (Italian version). (Paris)
$\frac{1851}{1885}$	El Correo de la Moda. (Madrid)

72　Summer Toilettes. Unsigned
From "Le Petit Courrier des Dames," May, 1851

74　Morning Toilettes. By A. de Taverne

From " Le Journal des Demoiselles," August, 1853

73　Summer Toilettes. Unsigned

From " Le Petit Courrier des Dames," August, 1852

$\frac{1851}{1879}$	Victoria. Illustrirte Muster- und Moden-Zeitung. (Berlin)
$\frac{1852}{1853}$	Le Bon Ton, Journal of Fashions (English version). (Paris)
$\frac{1852}{1877}$	The Englishwoman's Domestic Magazine. (London)
$\frac{1852}{189-}$	Le Journal des Dames et des Demoiselles. (Brussels)
$\frac{1852}{1855}$	La Bonne Compagnie. (Paris)
ca. 1852	Wiener Allgemeine-Zeitung. (Vienna)
$\frac{1852}{1865}$	Frauen-Zeitung für Hauswesen, Weibliche Arbeiten und Moden. (Stuttgart)
$\frac{1853}{1854}$	The Monitor of Fashion. (New York)
$\frac{1853}{1859}$	Wiener Moden-Spiegel. Wochenschrift für Mode, Schöne Literatur, Novellistik, Kunst und Theater. (Vienna)
$\frac{1853}{1858}$	Pariser Moden-Salon. Technische Zeitschrift für Damengarde-robe, Moden und Weibliche Arbeiten. (Berlin)
$\frac{1853}{1861}$	Penelope. Neue Muster-Zeitung für Weibliche Arbeiten und Moden. (Glogau)
ca. 1854	L'Élégant. (Paris)
$\frac{1854}{19-}$	Der Bazar (also Dutch and Italian versions). (Berlin)
$\frac{1854}{1855}$	La Revue Universelle, Journal de l'Aristocratie. (Paris)
$\frac{1854}{1871}$	Frank Leslie's Ladies Gazette of Fashion. (New York)

ca. 1855	Berliner Moden- und Muster-Zeitung. (Berlin)
$\frac{1855}{1878}$	Le Moniteur des Dames et des Demoiselles. (Paris)
$\frac{1855}{1857}$	Le Progrès. (Dresden)
$\frac{1856}{1862}$	La Mode Nouvelle. (Paris)
$\frac{1856}{1862}$	L'Abeille Impériale, Littérature, Poésie, Beaux-Arts, Théâtres. Messager des Modes et de l'Industrie. (Paris)
$\frac{1856}{1858}$	Hermann Gersons Mode-Zeitung. (Berlin)
ca. 1856	Le Progrès, Bulletin of Fashion. (New York)
$\frac{1856}{1882}$	Le Monde Élégant, Estafette des Modes. (Paris)
ca. 1858	Nouveautés de Paris. (Paris)
$\frac{1858}{1895}$	The Ladies' Treasury. (London)
$\frac{1859}{1873}$	La Toilette de Paris. (Paris)
$\frac{1859}{1882}$	La Mode de Paris. (Paris)
$\frac{1860}{1862}$	O Mensageiro das Damas. (Lisbon)
$\frac{1860}{19-}$	La Mode Illustrée. (Paris)
$\frac{1861}{1874}$	L'Illustrateur des Dames et des Demoiselles, Journal des Soirées de Famille. (Paris)

$\dfrac{1861}{19—}$ The Queen. (London)

$\dfrac{1862}{1864}$ The Paris Elegant and Journal of Fashion. (London)

$\dfrac{1862}{1864}$ Revue des Modes et de l'Industrie de Paris. (Paris)

$\dfrac{1864}{19—}$ The Young Ladies' Journal. (London)

$\dfrac{1865}{1866}$ Csaladi Kor. (Budapest)

$\dfrac{1865}{1886}$ Die Damen-Toilette. (Berlin)

$\dfrac{1865}{1897}$ Bow Bells. (London)

$\dfrac{1865}{19—}$ Die Modenwelt. Illustrirte Zeitung für Toilette und Hand-arbeiten. (Berlin). Foreign editions of Die Modenwelt appeared in many countries, of which the following is a complete list (with their regional titles):

Paris—La Saison	Holland—De Bazar
London—The Season	Russia—Modnii Svyet
New York—The Season	Denmark—Dagmar
Italy—La Stagione	Poland—Tygodnik Mod
Spain—La Estacion	Hungary—Budapesti Bazar
Portugal—A Estaçâo	Sweden—Freja
Czech—Modni Svet	

$\dfrac{1865}{1877}$ The Young Englishwoman. (London). *Later* Sylvia's Home Journal

$\dfrac{1866}{1876}$ L'Aquarelle-Mode. Compositions. Nouveautés. (Paris)

1868	Il Giornale delle Famiglie. (Milan)
$\frac{1869}{19—}$	La Mode Artistique. Recueil de Modes Nouvelles Coloriées et Gouachées à l'Aquerelle. (Paris)
$\frac{1869}{1875}$	La Novità. (Milan)
$\frac{1870}{1894}$	Wedding Bells. A Journal for the Single and Married of the U.K. (London)
$\frac{1870}{1874}$	Dress and Fashion. (London)
$\frac{1870}{1881}$	The Milliner and Dressmaker and Warehouseman's Gazette. (London)

* * * * *

The following are the periodicals from the two previous lists which overlap into the present period. The years of their first publication are given in brackets.

Allgemeine Moden-Zeitung (1799)
Zeitung für die Elegante Welt (1801)
La Belle Assemblée (1806)
Wiener Moden-Zeitung (1816)
Le Petit Courrier des Dames (1822)
Townsend's Monthly Selection (1823)
The World of Fashion (1824)
Der Spiegel für Kunst (1828)
Le Follet (1829)
La Mode (1829)
Godey's Ladies' Book (1830)
Berliner Modenspiegel (1832)
Journal des Jeunes Personnes (1832)
Ladies' Cabinet of Fashions (1832)
Le Voleur (1832)

75   Blind Man's Buff. By A. de Taverne

From "Le Petit Courrier des Dames," July, 1854

76   Evening Dresses. Engraved by Hopwood after E. Préval
From "Le Journal des Demoiselles," January, 1853

77 Indoor Dresses. Engraved by G. de Montaut after Compte-Calix

From "Les Modes Parisiennes," 1855

78 Summer Dresses. Engraved by G. de Montaut after Compte-Calix

From "Les Modes Parisiennes," 1855

79 Afternoon Dresses. Engraved by A. Bodry after Jules David

From "Le Journal des Dames et des Demoiselles," March, 1856

80 Winter Fashions for children. Engraved by E. Guérard after Compte-Calix

From "Les Modes Parisiennes," 1856

81   Theatre Dresses. By Anaïs Toudouze
From " Le Follet," 1857

83 Chambéry Gauze Dress with eight flounces.
Organdie tea-gown with a cape. Engraved by
A. Portier after A. Pauquet

From "Le Journal des Demoiselles," September, 1859

82 Visiting and House Dresses. Engraved by A. Portier
after A. Pauquet

From "Le Journal des Demoiselles," November, 1858

84   The Latest Fashions. Walking, Riding and Visiting Dresses. By Jules David
From "The Englishwoman's Domestic Magazine," August, 1860

85 Taffetta Day Dress and antique
moiré dress. Engraved by
A. Portier after A. Pauquet
*From "Le Journal des Demoiselles,"
December, 1861*

86 Indian Foulard Dress
and alpaca Visiting
Dress. Unsigned; pro-
bably by A. Pauquet
*From "Le Journal des Demoi-
selles," September, 1862*

87　Even children wear crinolines. By Anaïs Toudouze
From " Le Follet," 1863

88   Evening Toilettes. By Anaïs Toudouze

From " Le Follet," 1863

89   Country Dresses. Engraved by
E. Bracquet after Compte-Calix

From " Les Modes Parisiennes," 1863

90   Country Dresses. Engraved by
Louis Berlier after Héloïse Leloir

From " La Belle Assemblée," July, 1864

91   Garden Toilettes. Engraved by Barreau
after Laure Noël

From " La Musée des Familles," July, 1865

93   Country Dresses. Engraved by A. Lacourrière
after Compte-Calix
From "Les Modes Parisiennes," 1867

92   Afternoon and Evening Dresses. Unsigned
From "Le Petit Courrier des Dames," 1866

94   Seaside Costumes. Engraved by Huard after Anaïs Toudouze
From " La Mode Illustrée," July, 1868

95   Garden Dresses. Engraved by A. Carrache after Compte-Calix

From " Les Modes Parisiennes," July, 1869

96   Wedding Dresses. By Isabelle Toudouze

From " Le Monde Élégant," September, 1870

97   Wedding Dress and Afternoon Dress. Unsigned. Probably by Jules David

From " The Englishwoman's Domestic Magazine," November, 1870

98   Latest Paris Fashions. Unsigned

From " The Young Ladies of Great Britain," February, 1871

The above two plates are inferior ones produced outside France during the Siege of Paris, 1870–1871

Le Journal des Demoiselles (1833)
La Musée des Familles (1833)
Le Bon Ton (1834)
Psyche (1834)
Europa (1835)
Longchamps et Paris Élégant (1836)
Le Caprice (1836)
La Sylphide (1839)
Pariser Moden-Journal (1839)
Dziennik Domowy (1840)
L'Oriflamme des Modes (1840)
Le Journal des Femmes (1840)
Graham's Magazine (1841)
El Correo del Ultramar (1841)
Die Elegante (1842)
Jahreszeiten (1842)
La Moda Elegante Illustrada (1842)
The Ladies' Gazette of Fashion (1842)

CHAPTER SIX

The Fourth Period: 1871—1899

WE now come to the last period of the Victorian fashion-plate, the period in which it declined and deteriorated, as mechanical colour-printing began to get a strangle-hold on fashion magazines. Women's clothing had begun to lose much of its charm towards the end of the 1860s. The crinoline, which had reached its greatest circumference in 1859, started to wither in 1860. Instead of billowing out from the waist, it went straight down to the ground at an angle of sixty degrees (Fig. 84). In outdoor garments this line started from the shoulders; the spread of the dress first disappeared from the front; it is sometimes maintained that the crinoline of the 1850s had been designed at the instigation of the Empress Eugénie to enable her to appear at public functions at the latest possible date before the arrival of her son, the Prince Imperial. Then, for a short time, between 1866 and 1868, young ladies exposed their ankles, particularly in the summer, in a way which I feel must thoroughly have shocked their mothers and recalled the reckless 'thirties to their grandmothers.

By the end of 1868 the crinoline had entirely disappeared and had given way to the bustle. Historians declare that the real reason for the disappearance of the crinoline was the advent of the hansom-cab. The really smart lady with dashing ambition longed above all to ride in a hansom-cab, in which it was considered to be fast, in more ways than one, to ride; but, alas! with a crinoline this was an ambition almost impossible to achieve, unless one altered the position of that apparatus from the horizontal to the vertical, which would have entailed the exposure of a good deal more feminine lingerie than even a present-day miss would risk. So the crinoline had to go, at any rate for the young, though it lingered on for older ladies until near the end of the century and we enter the 1870s and what I like to call the era of ribbons, frills and flounces; a glance at Figs. 99, 100, 101, 103 will show what I mean.

For the first six years of the 1870s fashions still held a great deal of romance. It was the period during which James Tissot painted many of the most attractive of his pictures, which depend for their charm very largely upon the fashion of the period.

Then suddenly, in the middle of 1876, something seemed to happen to the fashion designers, and feminine costume became hideous and ridiculous and must have been excruciatingly uncomfortable. Even the children suffered; think of a modern child being asked to wear the clothes suggested in the April number of *The Queen* in 1876 (Plate V).

But to go back for a year, look at this quaint picture from *Le Follet* of two ladies apparently adrift in a boat which seems to be really too small for both of them (Fig. 103). It was drawn in 1875 by Isabelle Toudouze who, good fashion-plate artist though she was, cannot have known much about the sea. It is a little difficult to understand how the ladies reached their precarious position. Their craft has no rowlocks, no oars and no rudder. There is a rope hanging into the water from the side of the boat; the object of it is obscure, as, if it was meant to have an anchor at the end of it, it would have to be straining either fore or aft, whichever end that might be; so we must presume that it is only put into the picture for effect, and to add to the general nautical atmosphere. Perhaps the most charming thing about the drawing is the complete calm and imperturbability of the ladies, who with the customary serenity of ladies in fashion-plates, do not seem to be aware of their predicament or to realise how remote are their chances of ever reaching shore again without the aid of a lifeboat. In any case, the idea of a lady on the high seas with a parasol in one hand and a fan in the other, and wearing a dress which might be thought a little elaborate for a London garden-party, makes a definite appeal to the imagination.

It is no part of the object of this book to discuss fashions, so the foregoing remarks are really rather in the nature of a digression. They are, however, necessary for the narrative, so that the difficulties and the disappointments of the prevailing fashions with which the fashion-plate artists of the period had to struggle may be understood. New artists were beginning to come into the field, but they must have looked back with regret to the 1840s and 1850s with their lovely crinolines and flounces.

The Merveilleuses, with their "Incroyables", had passed, so had the Lionnes and the Romantiques, and the next phase was to be the Mondaines, who came along in the late 1880s and survive to this day. But the 1880s were now approaching, that terrible period which reached its culmination of ugliness in 1886 and 1887, with its severe, sombre, slightly tailor-made look and the bonnets which I once described in another book as giving the women the appearance of crayfish. No wonder the Pre-Raphaelite Brotherhood revolted against it and clad their women in long, flowing, wide-sleeved garments, and portrayed them in the same way in their pictures.

Just consider three typical fashion-plates of these two years, taken from the best magazines of their time, two from the *Revue de la Mode* (1872–1888) and one from *l'Art et la Mode* (1880–1900) (Figs. 111 to 113). It is difficult to think of what to say about them. In Fig. 111 the dress worn by the lady on the left has nothing whatever to recommend it; it has neither style nor line nor charm of any sort; in fact it is simply an abomination. About the lady in the evening waistcoat, Eton jacket and the tie, the less said the better. In the second picture from the *Revue de la Mode* the ladies are a little more feminine, though it seems to be rather a mystery how they ever got into the clothes they are wearing. They are presumably preparing to play lawn tennis. I wonder what a modern lady lawn-tennis champion would have thought of their costumes and their racquets. The third lady, from *l'Art et la Mode*, I present without comment; I doubt whether any comment that would really do it justice is possible.

Some years ago I was staying with friends in the country when an old lady came to tea and complained of the dresses of the day. When she was married, she explained, the clothes women wore were so elegant and beautiful. And, in answer to my question, she said that she had been married in 1886. It so happened that I had brought with me, for the purpose of study, a volume of *La Mode Illustrée* for that very year. I handed

Children's Dresses at the height of the Crinoline Period. By Francois-Claudins Compte-Calix

From "Les Modes Parisiennes," 1860

PLATE IV

PLATE V

Fashions of 1876
From "The Queen," April 1876

99   Afternoon Toilettes. Engraved
by Bonnard after E. Préval
*From Frank Leslie's "Lady's Magazine"
(New York), 1871*

100   Reception Toilettes.
Engraved by Bonnard
after Jules David
*From "Le Moniteur de la Mode,"
1872*

101 Afternoon Dresses. Engraved by E. Cheffer after G. Gonin
From "Wedding Bells," July, 1874

102   Walking Dresses. Engraved by Bonnard after Jules David

From the " Die Allgemeine Moden-Zeitung," Leipzig, 1875

103   Boating Costume. Engraved by Huard
      after Isabelle Toudouze

From " Le Follet," 1875

105   Fashionable Toilettes from Italy. Unsigned
From "Margherita, Giornale delle Signore Italiane," Milan, December, 1878

104   The Newest French Fashions. By P. Deferneville
From "The Ladies' Treasury," 1877

106   Riding Habit and Walking Dress. Engraved by Tailhaud after Jules David
From the "Société des Journaux de Mode Réunis," 1879

107　The Latest Paris Fashions. Unsigned
From " The Queen," February, 1881

109   Seaside Toilettes. Signed Poulet
From " The Queen," June, 1883

108   River Dresses. By Lefranco
From " Le Salon de la Mode," June, 1882

110 Walking Dresses for the Bois de Boulogne. Engraved by A. Portier after E. Mille

From "La Mode Actuelle," 1884

111 Indoor Toilettes. Engraved by A. Chaillot after A. Sandoz

From "La Revue de la Mode," 1886

112 The Lawn-Tennis Party. By P. Deferneville

From "La Revue de la Mode," 1887

113 Walking Dress. By Marie de Solar

From "L'Art et la Mode," 1887

it to her, and she looked carefully through it; then she commented: "I don't believe a word of it; this must be some kind of joke; our clothes were never at all like this." And she was quite angry about it.

Better times were, however, ahead, and already by 1889 an improvement began to appear (Fig. 116). By 1893 there was a swing back to the more romantic clothes of thirty years before. I would like to call particular attention to a charming plate which appeared in this year in *Le Moniteur de la Mode* (Fig. 121). Jules David had died the year before, and his mantle had fallen on G. Gonin, who was well qualified to carry on the tradition of the magazine. The plate in question shows two ladies in conversation over tea. They are so earnest and yet so calm, and for some reason they make me think of what Du Maurier or even Whistler would have done if they had ever designed fashion-plates.

The year 1895 produced some of the most elegant fashions of this last period. Soft pastel colours had taken the place of the dull browns, maroons and blacks of the 1880s; the bonnet had yielded to the wide-brimmed hat, and huge leg-of-mutton sleeves, reminiscent of the 1830s, but of better shape, gave a helpless but very feminine line to the fashions (Fig. 124). This fashion persisted, with slight variations, until the end of the century, when the general scramble started among the Fashion Dictators of Paris, a struggle which has been going on ever since. My history of fashion-plates stops at 1899 because during the past fifty years the history of fashion and fashion magazines has been almost as complicated as the history of mankind itself, and I leave it to posterity to unravel.

During the period dealt with in the last chapter (1843–1870), at least a hundred new fashion magazines, most of them known to have issued coloured fashion-plates, appeared in Europe. There were probably many others which were so ephemeral that no record of them has survived. Odd fashion-plates often turn up of which no trace can be found in any catalogue of any national library. I have, for instance, one isolated plate in my possession which is definitely of the fashions of 1871. It represents two ladies in not very inspiring clothes, and bears the caption "Latest Paris Fashions. Presented gratis with the February part of *The Young Ladies of Great Britain*" (Fig. 98). For years this puzzled me until one day I discovered that it was a sequel to another magazine, called *Dress and Fashion*, published in 1870 and 1871, probably as a stopgap during the Franco-Prussian War.

In this last period comparatively few new fashion magazines made their appearance, but many of them were of considerable importance. The most noteworthy were *La Revue de la Mode* (1872–1888), the *Illustrirte Frauen-Zeitung* (Berlin 1874–19—), which had a very wide Continental circulation, *La Mode Actuelle* (*ca.* 1880) and *Wiener Mode*, one of the most elegant of all the later fashion magazines, which appeared first in Vienna in 1887 and carried on well into the present century. *La Mode Actuelle* seems to have been published in London, or at any rate to have had a London edition. Of other magazines originating in London in this period, the most important was *Myra's Journal of Dress and Fashion* (1875–1893). This paper, in 1875, issued the largest fashion-plate I have ever seen; it measures approximately thirty inches by twelve inches and contains reproductions of fourteen other plates. An odd fact is that no new magazines seem to have appeared between 1894 and 1899.

I conclude this parade of fashion-plates with two that are typical of the end of the century. The first, from *The Young Ladies' Journal* of 1898, is a coloured lithograph of three ladies about to set out on a nice afternoon's bicycle ride; I wonder what they would have thought of the young ladies one sees speeding along the Great West Road on a fine Summer afternoon nowadays. They would probably have called a policeman! The second plate, from the *Journal des Dames et des Demoiselles*, a magazine which dated from 1852, is interesting as being one of the last plates to be coloured by hand; it was issued in 1899, an uncomfortable year when even little girls were forced to try to choke themselves with high, tight collars.

Fashion Periodicals : 1871—1899

Hand-list of the principal periodicals with coloured fashion-plates which first appeared during the period covered by the foregoing chapter, namely, 1871–1899, together with the years during which they were published.

* * * * * *

$\dfrac{1871}{1872}$	The Young Ladies of Great Britain.
$\dfrac{1871}{1875}$	Les Modes de la Saison. (Paris)
$\dfrac{1872}{1874}$	The Month's Dress and Fashion. *Sequel to* The Young Ladies of Great Britain. (London)
$\dfrac{1872}{1875}$	La Modiste Élégante. (Paris)
$\dfrac{1872}{1888}$	La Revue de la Mode. (Paris)
$\dfrac{1872?}{1885}$	Journal le Printemps. (Paris)
$\dfrac{1873}{?}$	La Mode Élégante. Modes de Paris, Littérature, Illustrations, Beaux-Arts, etc.
$\dfrac{1874}{1879}$	Le Conseiller des Familles. Littérature, Travaux à l'Aiguille, Modes, etc. (Paris)
1874	La Modiste Parisienne. (Paris)
$\dfrac{1874}{1885}$	La Mode Universelle. Journal Illustré des Dames. (Paris)
$\dfrac{1874}{19—}$	Illustrirte Frauen-Zeitung. (Berlin)

$\dfrac{1875}{1893}$ Myra's Journal of Dress and Fashion. (London)

$\dfrac{1875}{1894}$ La Mode Française. (Paris)

$\dfrac{1876}{1897}$ La Modiste Universelle. (Paris)

$\dfrac{1876}{19-}$ Le Salon de la Mode. (Paris) *and* Spanish edition El Salon de la Moda. (Madrid)

$\dfrac{1877}{1886}$ L'Avenir de la Mode. (Paris)

$\dfrac{1877}{1884}$ Paris Charmant Artistique. (Paris)

$\dfrac{1878}{?}$ The Illustrated Household Journal and Englishwoman's Domestic Magazine. (London). *Sequel to* the Englishwoman's Domestic Magazine, 1852–1877

$\dfrac{1878}{1894}$ Sylvia's Home Journal. (London)

$\dfrac{1878}{1887}$ Margherita, Giornale delle Signore Italiane. (Milan)

$\dfrac{1879}{1881}$ Berliner Modenblatt. (Berlin)

$\dfrac{1879}{1894}$ Ebhardts Moden-Album. (Berlin)

$\dfrac{1879}{19-}$ Le Petit Echo de la Mode. (Paris)

ca. 1880 La Mode Actuelle. (London)

$\dfrac{1880}{1888}$ Il Tesoro delle Famiglie. (Milan)

$\frac{1880}{19-}$	L'Art et la Mode. (Paris)
$\frac{1882}{1889}$	Le Moniteur de la Mode, a Fashionable Journal appearing monthly. (London). *Sequel to* Milliner and Dressmaker
$\frac{1882}{1883}$	La Vie Élégante. (Paris)
$\frac{1885}{19-}$	Mode und Haus, Praktische Illustrirte Frauen-Zeitung. (Berlin)
1885	Le Courrier Mondain. (Paris)
ca. 1886	Le Journal des Enfants. (Paris)
ca. 1886	La Nouveauté. (Paris)
$\frac{1886}{1894}$	Revue des Modes Parisiennes. (Paris)
$\frac{1887}{?}$	The Lady's World. (London)
ca. 1887.	La Toilette Moderne. (Paris)
ca. 1887.	La Gazette des Femmes. (Paris)
$\frac{1887}{19-}$	Wiener Mode. (Vienna)
ca. 1887 $\frac{}{1895}$	Le Luxe. Grande Édition Parisienne. Société Générale des Journaux Professionels des Couturières et Confectionneuses. (Paris)
$\frac{1889}{1890}$	Divat-Tükör. (Budapest)
$\frac{1890}{19-}$	Die Elegante Mode. (Berlin)
ca. 1890	Société des Journaux et des Modes Réunies. (Paris)

$\dfrac{1891}{19-}$ Leipziger Moden-Zeitung. (Leipzig)

$\dfrac{1891}{19-}$ Wiener Chic. (Vienna)

$\dfrac{1892}{19-}$ Die Grosse Modenwelt. (Berlin)

$\dfrac{1892}{19-}$ La Mode Pratique. (Paris)

$\dfrac{1892}{1894}$ Fashions of Today (English version of La Mode Pratique). (Paris)

ca. 1893   Élégances Parisiennes. (Paris) ⎤ amalgamated in 1894 with Le

ca. 1893   La Gazette Rose. (Paris)   ⎦   Moniteur de la Mode

$\dfrac{1894}{19-}$ La Nouvelle Mode. (Paris)

ca. 1899.   Chic Parisien. (Paris)

*   *   *   *   *   *

The following are the periodicals from the three previous lists which overlap into the present period. The years of their first appearance are given in brackets.

Allgemeine Moden-Zeitung (1799)
Townsend's Monthly Selections (1823)
Le Follet (1829)
Godey's Ladies' Handbook (1830)
La Musée des Familles (1833)
Le Journal des Demoiselles (1833)
Le Bon Ton (1834)
Europa (1835)
Jahreszeiten (1842)
La Moda Elegante Illustrada (1842)

The Ladies' Gazette of Fashion (1842)
Le Moniteur de la Mode (1843)
Les Modes Parisiennes (1844)
Le Magazin des Demoiselles (1844)
The Gazette of Fashion (1846)
El Correo de la Moda (1851)
Victoria (1851)
Le Journal des Dames et des Demoiselles (1852)
The Englishwoman's Domestic Magazine (1852)
Le Moniteur des Dames et des Demoiselles (1855)
Der Bazar (1855)
Le Monde Élégant (1856)
The Ladies' Treasury (1858)
La Toilette de Paris (1859)
La Mode de Paris (1859)
La Mode Illustrée (1860)
L'Illustrateur des Dames et des Demoiselles (1861)
The Queen (1861)
The Young Ladies' Journal (1864)
Die Damen-Toilette (1865)
Bow Bells (1865)
Die Modenwelt, and its foreign editions (1865)
The Young Englishwoman (1865)
L'Aquarelle-Mode (1866)
La Mode Artistique (1869)
Dress and Fashion (1870)
The Milliner and Dressmaker (1870)
Wedding Bells (1870)

CHAPTER SEVEN

The Artists

WHEN I set out to write the story of the nineteenth-century fashion-plates, one of the objects that I had in view was to tell about the artists who were responsible for them. But, unfortunately, little remains of the majority of them except their names and their work. This is true of so many artists whose lives are absorbed in their work and who have, therefore, little time for extraneous activities. What, for instance, is known of the private lives of Velasquez or Boucher? Practically nothing. There have, of course, been artists who have led colourful and adventurous lives, like Goya, Gavarni and many of the modern popular painters, but they are exceptions.

There was one family, however, which I cannot let lapse into oblivion, namely, that of Alexandre-Marie Colin, a painter and lithographer, who was born in 1798 and died in 1875. Colin was quite a distinguished artist in his day and was the father of three daughters who were responsible for many of the most charming fashion-plates of the mid-nineteenth century.

The eldest, Héloïse, was born in 1820. She married a painter named Leloir, and all her plates are signed with her married name, Héloïse Leloir. She designed plates for the house of Mariton, which were distributed to many French magazines and were also issued with *La Belle Assemblée* from 1855 until it ceased publication in 1868. Héloïse died in 1874.

The second daughter, Adèle Anaïs, was born in 1822 and lived until 1899. She married, in 1845, G. A. Toudouze, and nearly all her plates are signed Anaïs Toudouze, though early plates of hers, in 1844, can be found signed Anaïs Colin. She was the most industrious of the three

114   Children's Fashions for the Seaside. Engraved by Huard after Alice Dupan
From "Le Journal des Enfants," 1886

115   Seaside Costumes. By A. Sandoz
From "The Queen," August, 1888

117   Walking Dresses. By A. Sandoz.
From "The Queen," May, 1890

116   Summer Dresses. Engraved by A. Portier after Jules David
From "Le Moniteur de la Mode," June, 1889

118   Fancy Dress (Paris Exhibition) 1890. Signed B. C.
Probably from "Le Journal des Demoiselles"

sisters and drew continuously for a number of French magazines. Examples of her work can be seen in Figs. 67, 87, 88, 94.

When Anaïs Toudouze ceased drawing fashion-plates, which she appears to have done in about 1875, she passed the torch on to her daughter Isabelle, whose delicate plates for *Le Follet* (which were also issued with *The Queen*) had already been appearing for some years in other papers. Isabelle inherited the best traditional fashion-plate technique from her mother (Figs. 96, 103).

Colin's third daughter was Laure, born in 1827. Her plates are nearly all signed with her married name, Laure Noël, and were drawn principally for *La Musée des Familles*, *La Mode Illustrée* and *Le Journal des Demoiselles*. As I have already mentioned, some early fashion-plates of hers can be found signed with her maiden name, Laure Colin (Fig. 66).

A complete collection of the Colin family fashion-plates, added to those of Gavarni and of Jules David, would form a perfect review of fashion from 1830 until over sixty years later.

There were many very fine fashion-plate artists who never signed their plates, particularly the early artists of *La Belle Assemblée* and *The Repository of Arts*. One of the earliest signatures we have is that of William Hopwood, who signed his plates for *The Lady's Magazine* in the 1820s (Fig. 37). There were other artists who signed their drawings but who were not very regular contributors; these must be taken on their merits. But I think that the best help I can give to the intending collector is to give a list, in alphabetical order, of the artists who contributed regularly to fashion magazines, who signed their drawings and whose work should be sought for and acquired whenever possible. As an additional guide, I have given, against their names, the main periodicals in which most of their work appeared. If one keeps to this list, it would be difficult to go very far wrong.

ALAIS, William Wolfe. Engraver. Exhibited in the Royal Academy in 1829 and 1833. Although his engravings were copies of French plates, they were tastefully executed for *The World of Fashion* in the 1820s.

BODIN, A. Engraver. Exhibited in the Paris Salon of 1861. Executed good plates for French magazines in the Third Period.

CARRACHE. One of the chief engravers of Compte-Calix's plates for *Les Modes Parisiennes*.

CLOSMENIL, Mme Florensa de. Sometimes signing herself simply Florensa. Her plates appeared in *Le Journal des Demoiselles*, *La Mode* and *Le Petit Courrier des Dames*.

COMTE-CALIX, François-Claudins. Principally in *Les Modes Parisiennes*, of which he was the chief artist, and also in *Le Petit Courrier des Dames*.

DAVID, JULES. Drew all the fashion-plates for *Le Moniteur de la Mode* from 1843 until 1892. These were also issued in many other magazines in Europe, including *The Englishwoman's Domestic Magazine*, *The Milliner and Dressmaker*, *The Young Englishwoman*, *Myra's Journal of Dress and Fashion* and the Berlin *Allgemeine Modenzeitung*.

GAVARNI. *La Mode*, *Psyché*, *La Sylphide*, *La Vogue*, *Le Voleur*, *Le Journal des Gens du Monde*, *Le Journal des Femmes*, *Le Journal des Jeunes Personnes* and *l'Abeille Impériale*.

GONIN, G. *Le Luxe*, *Le Moniteur de la Mode*, *The Queen*, *Myra's Journal*.

GOURDON, E. *The Young Englishwoman*, *La Mode Actuelle*.

GUÉRARD, E. *La Mode*, *Les Modes Parisiennes*.

HERVY. *Le Petit Courrier des Dames*.

HUCHOT, V. *Le Beau Monde*, *Le Journal le Printemps*.

JANET, Gustave. *La Mode Artistique*, *Le Mode Illustrée* and *La Revue de la Mode*. He was the brother of Janet Lange, another outstanding fashion-plate designer.

L., Nelly. I know no more of her than this, which was the signature she used on her plates. Her work was mostly lithographic and she made some very pretty plates for *Le Journal des Femmes*, *Les Modes de Paris* and the *Tribune Dramatique*.

LANGE, Janet. One of the earliest fashion-plate artists to produce "conversation pieces" in this sphere. Her plates are to be found in *Le Voleur*, *La Mode*, *La Sylphide* and *Le Cabinet de Lecture*.

LANTÉ, Louis-Marie. Drew some outstanding fashion-plates for *La Mode*, *La Sylphide*, *Le Journal des Dames et des Modes* and *Le Petit Modiste*

Français. Born in 1789, he was one of the best of the fashion-plate designers and was closely associated with Horace Vernet. In his early days he designed plates for *Le Journal des Modes* (1817).

LELOIR, Héloïse. Daughter of Alexandre Colin; already referred to earlier.

LELOUP, Amélie. Designed hats for *Le Follet*.

MILLE, E. One of the best of the later artists of *Le Follet*.

MONTAUT, Gabriel-Xavier. Draughtsman and engraver. Executed many plates for *La Revue des Modes de Paris*, *Le Petit Courrier des Dames* and *Les Modes Parisiennes*.

MOUTET, C. Some very fine plates for *Le Journal le Printemps*, *Le Follet* and *The Queen* (1876).

NOËL, Laure. Already referred to among the Colin family. She drew for *La Musée des Familles*, *La Mode Illustrée*, *Le Journal des Demoiselles* and *Le Follet*.

NUMA. A mysterious person of whom, in spite of lengthy research, I have been able to discover nothing. His plates appeared for some years in the 1830s and 1840s, in a dozen papers, including *La Mode*, *La Sylphide*, *Le Miroir des Dames*, *L'Avenir*, *L'Aspic* and *Psyché*. He, or she, was one of the finest fashion-plate artists of that period. "Numa" may well have been an alias of some famous artist who wished to keep this particular activity of his anonymous. Perhaps someone will be able to unravel the mystery.

PAUQUET, A. Very stylish, but a little stylised, drawings for *Le Petit Courrier des Dames*, *Le Journal des Demoiselles* and *The Queen*.

PRÉVAL, E. One of the most prolific of the artists of the 1860s. His plates appeared in most of the best magazines of the period, including *Le Journal des Demoiselles*, *Les Modes Parisiennes*, *Le Petit Courrier des Dames*, *The Young Englishwoman*, *The Queen* and *Der Bazar*. Préval was by turns a draughtsman and an engraver.

SANDOZ, A. Excellent plates for *The Queen* from 1888 until 1898.

SETE, Bertha. I have seen only one fashion-plate from her brush, and it had no caption, but I wish I could see some more.

SOLAR, Marie de. Excellent plates in *L'Art et la Mode* and *Le Courrier Mondain.* Among the best of those of the end of the century.

TAVERNE, A. de. Attractive plates from the 1850s onwards in *Le Journal des Demoiselles* and *Le Petit Courrier des Dames*; and later on for *The Queen.* Often signed A. de Txxxxxx.

THIRION, E. Starting in the 1870s, he drew principally for *Le Journal le Printemps.* His plates also appeared regularly in English fashion magazines, notably *The Lady's Treasury, The Young Englishwoman* and *Myra's Journal.*

TOUDOUZE, Anaïs (née Colin). One of the most prolific and certainly the most popular of all the later fashion-plate artists. At various times her work appeared in at least twenty of the best magazines, the principal ones, in which the plates were first issued, being *Le Follet, Le Magasin des Demoiselles* and *La Mode Illustrée.*

TOUDOUZE, Isabelle. Daughter of Anaïs. Contributed plates to *Le Follet, Le Monde Élégant* and *The Queen.*

* * * * * *

The above list does not pretend to contain the names of all the artists who signed their plates, but it contains all the more important ones; to have listed them all would have been confusing.

The nineteenth-century fashion-plate artists worked in obscurity and I have no doubt that their work was very poorly paid by modern standards. Such as it was, it has survived, and many of the artists' names will live in the minds of students of fashion and collectors of fashion-plates long after the names of many hundreds of successful exhibitors of paintings in the salons and academies of their respective countries have been completely forgotten. They were a race apart.

CHAPTER EIGHT

Forming a Collection

SOME years ago two articles of mine on the subject of collecting fashion-plates were published, with an interval of seven years between them; the first appeared in 1931, the second in 1938. There were some errors and a great many omissions in both these articles, particularly in the first, as I was writing from my own experiences and not from research; I was also the first person, in England at any rate, to attempt to analyse and co-ordinate fashion-plates as such. In the present book I have tried to repair these errors and omissions, though I have little doubt that I will have a great many more pointed out to me.

There are two main works in which periodicals containing fashion-plates are catalogued in separate lists. The first of these is entitled, with typical German long-windedness, *Der Katalog der Freiherrlich von Lipperheidischen Kostümbibliotek*, to which I have already referred in my Introduction; it is usually referred to shortly as *Lipperheide*. This imposing work was published in Berlin in parts, between 1896 and 1905, and is a catalogue of books on all kinds of costume, as well as books that might have a bearing, however remote, on the subject. It is unfortunately limited by the fact that it only records books actually in Lipperheide's own library, and cannot therefore claim to be anything like a complete list. It does not, for instance, make any mention of either *The English-woman's Domestic Magazine* or *The Queen*, two of the most important of the English fashion magazines. However, it was the first book to attempt anything of the kind and as such is essential to the student of the fashion-plate.

Lipperheide's catalogue contains nearly 1500 pages and records over 5000 publications. Only twenty-five pages are devoted to fashion publications, and these pages deal with 225 publications, in chronological order

155

and comprising about 3350 volumes in all. A great many of the items are not fashion magazines at all, but are included because they are topical papers which throw light on the period during which they were published; there are, for instance, long, but incomplete runs of *Punch* and *The Illustrated London News*. German and Austrian magazines predominate in this collection; but this is to be expected, as the entire collection was formed in Germany; and less than half the periodicals listed contain the coloured plates which are the subject of the present study. It does not give the names of any artists, nor does it give the number of plates issued by each publication, or how often it was issued.

The other work is *La Bibliographie Générale du Costume et de la Mode*, by René Colas. This is more up-to-date than *Lipperheide*, having been published in Paris in 1933; this bibliography aims at listing all fashion magazines and does not confine itself to the contents of any particular library. It is based very largely on *Lipperheide*, but oddly enough it omits quite a number of the items in that catalogue; being a French publication, it naturally contains a large proportion of French magazines. But there are still a great number of gaps, *The Englishwoman's Domestic Magazine* and *The Queen* being again ignored. It is, however, a very useful book for the collector, as it gives far more details than *Lipperheide*.

Both these books are rare, but there are copies of them in The London Library and also in the Libraries of the British Museum and the Victoria and Albert Museum in South Kensington.

In the hand-lists which I have appended to Chapters III to VI I have included every publication mentioned in Lipperheide and Colas up to 1899 which issued coloured fashion-plates; and to these I have added a large number of other magazines, to the existence of which I can vouch from my own personal knowledge, as I have seen plates from every one of them. The lists are, therefore, more complete than any that have preceded them, so far as coloured fashion-plates are concerned.

To attempt, as Lipperheide did, to collect every book ever published on costume, is beyond either the means or the space available to most people, for such a collection would run into twenty or thirty thousand volumes. Even a collection of weekly or monthly fashion magazines would soon become embarrassingly large. One can, however, collect the loose hand-coloured plates issued with the fashion magazines; and a collection of these, however extensive, will, if neatly arranged in files or cabinets, occupy comparatively little space. The scope of collecting these plates is also limited. We have seen that the earliest true fashion-plates were issued towards the end of the eighteenth century. Until the early years of the nineteenth century these were not very numerous and often of poor quality. At the other end of the scale we find that by 1899 the hand-coloured fashion-plate had practically disappeared, surviving only in a few old-established magazines like *Le Journal des Demoiselles*.

The fashion-plate collector will no doubt eventually try to collect all the plates issued during the nineteenth century, but he would be well advised to start in a much less ambitious way, by concentrating at first upon a particular period. This is by far the most satisfactory method, as it gives the collector a nucleus on which to build. I suggest that a start should be made with a period of twenty years; when a thoroughly representative collection has been obtained for these years, a further ten years may be added to one end or the other, or to both; and as these are filled up, further extensions can be made. By a representative collection I mean at least fifty plates for each year, showing a variety of dresses for different occasions.

The year from which I would advise a start being made is 1850. There are several reasons for this. The plates from the earlier period (from 1800, or even earlier, to 1820) are difficult to get and are often in very poor condition. The period from 1821 to 1843 was a prolific one, but it produced mostly rather dull and uninspiring plates, with a few very rare exceptions; there are some amusing plates, but there are far more regrettable ones, particularly those of English and German origin; even the French plates, though often quaint, are often very monotonous in the sameness of their conception. But the period 1843 to 1870 is the golden age of the fashion-plate, when the artists vied with one another to produce such charming plates that it often seems that the dresses are subordinated to the pictures. So if one starts at 1850 and spreads up and down from that date, one is in the centre of the best years, and even if one does not spread very far one will have a collection which is well worth admiration and study.

At first it is easy to set a limit to oneself, but when a balanced collection has been formed from, let us say, 1840 to 1860, the temptation to overlap upwards into the 'sixties and downwards into the 'thirties becomes overwhelming; and before you know where you are you have dashed headlong into the 'seventies and are casting a covetous eye upon the 'eighties. But that is all part of the pleasure of the chase.

Another form of collecting is to collect only one type of plate: day dresses, evening dresses, walking dresses, or dresses designed for the country or the seaside. Bridal dresses form a particularly popular collection, as most of the foremost magazines issued one every three or six months, and it is easy to trace changes in fashion in them in a comparatively rapid manner.

Fancy dress in fashion-plates is a study entirely of its own. In the nineteenth century women had to be very circumspect and one of the few frivolous relaxations accorded to them was the cotillon and the fancy dress ball. So naturally the fashion magazines contained frequent suggestions for fancy dress. The earliest plates of any importance are those of Gavarni in *La Mode*. His "Travestissements" in that paper are classics and have been reproduced innumerable times. One interesting point about the fancy dress plate is that, whatever the date of the costume it represents, the basic design of the dress follows the prevailing fashion of the moment. The pierrette of the 1830s has sloping shoulders draped in a wide cape-like collar and a short skirt. The pierrette of the 1850s was a crinoline, and the one of the 1880s a bustle.

Fancy dresses also show a tendency to be topical; one of these is reproduced here; it comes from the collection of Mrs. Langley Moore and is one of the most amusing ones I know (Fig. 118). It was issued in 1890, probably with *Le Journal des Demoiselles*. It shows three figures, each representing some phase of the Paris Exhibition of that year. The first lady is a composite allegory of French interests in the Far and Middle East; there is an Egyptian and Libyan suggestion in her head-dress, and a slightly Indo-Chinese motif in the skirt and a peep of trousers beneath

158

119 Evening Toilettes. By A. Sandoz
From " The Queen," December, 1891

120 Country Dresses. Engraved
by A. Portier after G. Gonin
*From " Le Journal des Dames et des
Demoiselles," February, 1892*

121 Confidences. By G. Gonin
From " Le Moniteur de la Mode," December, 1893

122 Summer Dresses for children.
Unsigned

From "The Season," July, 1893

123 In the Bois de Boulogne. Engraved
by A. Portier after G. Gonin

From "Le Moniteur de la Mode," May, 1894

124 Promenade Dress. By H. Charles

From "La Mode Artistique," 1895

125 Afternoon Toilettes. By A. Sandoz

From "The Queen," October, 1896

it. The figure on the right can be nothing but a representation of the fire-works that were such a feature of the Exhibition. But the central figure is the most imposing, representing, as it does, the Eiffel Tower itself; I wonder if any lady ever had the temerity to have it made for her; certainly not unless she was very tall. Perhaps the most curious part of her costume is the wand, on the tip of which, prophetically, appears a television aerial!

And now for a word of warning. In his early enthusiasm the budding collector will seize upon almost every kind of plate that is offered to him, regardless of whether it be good or bad, so long as it fills a gap in his collection. But a very large proportion of the plates on the market are inferior ones, many being discards from other collections. These are easy to obtain and are comparatively cheap. Every period has produced a few outstanding fashion-plate artists whose work was copied by inferior craftsmen. Unfortunately this applies particularly to those English magazines of the middle periods which did not happen to import French plates. This is all the more unfortunate since these are, naturally, the plates most frequently encountered in England and are therefore the ones with which most collectors are tempted to make a start. If you succumb to this temptation, you may be sure that the original ones will turn up in due course, and then you will be faced with the painful duty of having to discard your early acquaintances.

I have already given fairly comprehensive lists of the magazines that contained the best plates; so I think it will be helpful to the collector to give a list of magazines commonly found, which should be avoided because of the inferiority of their plates. In that way the unwary may be helped to separate the sheep from the goats; I consider that I am justified in doing this, as most books dealing with collecting describe the sheep at great length, but ignore the goats entirely. It is so long since these magazines have ceased to exist that I have no fear of treading upon anyone's toes, particularly as none of the plates against which I am warning were ever signed by their artists' names. Avoid, then, at all costs:

La Belle Assemblée, from 1833 until 1854, except for a very brief period in 1836, when plates from *Le Follet* were imported from Paris. Before and after these two dates the plates are excellent.

The Ladies' Gazette of Fashion (1842–1894), already referred to.

Le Beau Monde, from about 1833, during the period in which it issued the same plates as the foregoing *Ladies' Gazette of Fashion*.

The Ladies' Pocket Magazine (1824–1840).

The World of Fashion (1824–1864), except for some of the earlier plates in the 1820s signed by William Alais. All the plates from this magazine were copies of French plates.

The Ladies' Cabinet of Fashions (1832–1870).

Many of the German and Austrian plates after 1840 should be avoided for the same reason, namely, that they are redrawn from French plates. Italian, Spanish and Portuguese periodicals, on the other hand, mostly imported French plates, with altered captions in their own languages; but these appeared weeks, and often months, after they had first appeared in the French magazines.

In the late 'eighties and the early 'nineties attempts were made by several magazines to produce fashion-plates by chromo-lithograph. This was seldom successful, and when the plates are found in their original magazines they are nearly always stuck to the opposite page. The earliest and most persistent of these came from Germany; the French seem never to have used this form of reproduction. Of the English ones, those in *Myra's Journal of Dress and Fashion* are the best known; they are quite awful, but are well worth collecting as curiosities.

One difficulty encountered by the would-be collector is that the nineteenth-century fashion magazines had an irritating habit, particularly in France, of suddenly changing their names. They were constantly amalgamating, in the most confusing manner. I have, for instance, seen copies of a magazine of 1887, calling itself *Le Petit Messager des Modes, La Corbeille, Le Courrier de la Mode, Le Monde Élégant et Les Nouveautés Parisiennes Réunies*. The magazine bears the dates 1843–1887, but there is nothing to suggest when the amalgamations took place. I have never seen a copy of *Le Courrier de la Mode*, or a plate from it, though it presumably existed or it would not have been mentioned; I have not included it in my lists, as there is nothing to show that it ever issued coloured fashion-plates of its own. I have seen only one plate from *La Corbeille*, a pretty one of children playing in a garden.

But all this is half the fun of collecting because, although one is constantly coming up against brick walls, one is also constantly making new discoveries and breaking fresh ground, and there is endless delight in poring over the foibles and pretty conceits of our very recent ancestors.

The study of fashion-plates in England is complicated by the fact that the fashion magazines in the National Collections are widely distributed, instead of being kept conveniently together. Today, the best public collection of fashion magazines is, without question, in the Victoria and Albert Museum in South Kensington; but there are many gaps in this collection. On the other hand, the British Museum in Bloomsbury possesses a number of magazines that would almost completely fill these gaps. Before the last war the British Museum had a very fine collection of fashion magazines, including long runs of *Les Modes Parisiennes*, *Le Journal des Demoiselles* and the *Moniteur de la Mode*. Unfortunately, however, nearly all these were destroyed by enemy action; but quite a number of fashion papers, including most of the English ones, have survived. A few of these are in London, but the majority of them are kept in the Newspaper Library at Colindale and are, consequently, very difficult of access. In particular, there is a long run of the English edition of *Le Follet*, which would cover a considerable gap in the Victoria and Albert Museum Library, to which it logically belongs. The useful value of these magazines would be greatly enhanced if they could be kept together, though at the moment of writing there seems to be no means by which this could be brought about.

There is one great point about collecting the coloured fashion-plates of the nineteenth century, and that is that it is conceivably possible to accumulate all those that are really worth while into one collection. As I have mentioned, my own collection at one time amounted to about 20,000 plates and contained most of the better ones, though I could have eliminated quite a considerable number without doing the collection any harm.

I consider that anyone who acquired 25,000 of the best would be able to sit back and relax. His collection would be, to all intents and purposes, complete.

Nineteenth-century fashion-plates are becoming rarer and rarer. A great many were destroyed during the last war, particularly in Germany, where there were some very fine collections. Most of the foreign fashion-magazines in the British Museum were also, as I have said, destroyed by enemy action. Again, film companies all over the world have formed large collections of fashion-plates to enable them to avoid the anachronisms in costume that characterised their earlier efforts; until about thirty years ago any lady in a film in which action was laid between 1820 and 1890 was always dressed in an 1857 dress and an 1837 hat. And there are all the arts and crafts shops which eagerly snap up coloured fashion-plates to use them for the decoration of lamp-shades, table-mats, trays and waste-paper baskets. Yet it is not even now too late to start, as every now and then one comes across "treasure-trove", as once happened to me when I discovered a twenty years' continuous run of *Les Modes Parisiennes* in a London antiquarian bookshop for £15; it contained over a thousand plates, including most of those ever drawn by Compte-Calix! Incidentally, it will still, oddly enough, be found cheaper to buy the complete magazines with all their plates, than to buy individual plates; I suppose that the reason for this is that, though a print-seller may nowadays price a good fashion-plate at 5s. to 7s. 6d., few booksellers would hope to get £15 or £20 for a bound volume containing sixty of them.

It is a common fallacy to think that age adds to the value of a fashion-plate. Until the 1840s, most fashion magazines were quite small, usually octavo or small octavo in size. In the 1840s they became larger and the prevailing size was quarto. The fashion-plates followed the sizes of the magazines with which they were issued. In the cases of the better magazines, a mass of extraneous material was included which was considered to be worthy of preservation, and, in consequence, bound volumes of them are common. When, however, the large folio weekly fashion magazine began to make its appearance, it was too large for most people to have bound and to place upon their shelves; so the majority of them were either destroyed or lay about and grew dustier and more frayed until they were eventually consigned to the merciful oblivion of the waste-paper basket. The later ones are consequently rarer, particularly if in good condition.

A very great deal can be done to improve the appearance of fashion-plates which have a shabby look about them. For the general cleaning of the plates the methods advised in any work on book-collecting should be studied. The substance known as "Art Cleanser", a very soft kind of eraser, should be used, very gently, for removing surface dust. If the edges are ragged or dirty, they should be trimmed, preferably with a large-sized photographic print-trimmer; this immensely improves their appearance, particularly if at any time they have been carelessly bound and need squaring up. If the white high-lights, particularly in bridal dresses, have changed to a dark brown, so that the pattern beneath can hardly be distinguished, the transparency can be restored by brushing the parts affected with the ordinary hydrogen peroxide to be obtained at any chemist's, and allowing them to dry; many booksellers are unaware of this, and one can often buy plates so disfigured at a nominal price, as rubbish.

The greatest real enemies of the fashion-plate are dust and foxing, so great care must be taken to preserve the collection from them, particularly in London. They should be kept in folders which are as dust-proof and damp-proof as possible; the folders themselves are best kept in filing cabinets, from which they can be easily referred to. One folder to each year should be enough, but separate folders, covering the whole period of the collection, should be set aside for certain very specialised costumes, such as bridal dresses, equestrian plates and riding costumes, archery dresses, children's dresses and fancy dress. Other categories will no doubt appeal to each collector.

* * * * * *

Collecting fashion-plates is a fascinating hobby and one which need not occupy much of one's time. Once one begins to take it seriously, it is very gratifying to find how many of one's friends have stray bound volumes of fashion magazines which they are eager to bestow upon one.

I remember H. G. Wells telling me that somewhere in his library he had two bound books of fashion-plates which I could have if I could find them. It took me a whole Summer afternoon and evening at Easton Glebe to find them, but I found them in the end; I forget what they were exactly, but I know that they made a valuable addition to my collection.

But, on the whole, I think that the main delight in collecting fashion-plates and fashion magazines is that they take you, not into the far-distant past, but into the immediate past of your recent forebears. And with them, as you muse over these plates, you can occasionally recapture the calm, the peace and the security of the days when a dictator was merely a master who gave dictation in a school.

NOTES ON SELECTED ILLUSTRATIONS

The Gallery of Fashion, June 1794

Plate I   A PEEP INTO KENSINGTON GARDENS

Morning Dresses

Left-hand seated figure. Straw-coloured gipsy hat, trimmed with a lilac riband formed into a large bow in front, and into a very small one behind; tied under the chin with a lilac-coloured silk handkerchief. One white and one lilac ostrich feather placed on the left side. The hair in light curls, falling down behind, bound with a white half-handkerchief, tied in the front into a large bow. Round gown of fine Indian calico, trimmed with a narrow flounce; long sleeves trimmed at the wrist with lace. Lilac-coloured sash tied into a small bow, the ends as long as the train. Lawn handkerchief, over it another of lilac-coloured silk, turned under the arms, and tied behind. Yellow shoes. Jonquille-coloured gloves.

Standing figure. Plain chip hat, trimmed with purple ribands. Hair lightly frizzed; chignon turned up in a loose plait. Plain muslin gown and petticoat. Short sleeves, trimmed at the elbows with lace. Full cravat round the neck. Small lawn handkerchief tied behind. Black silk cloak, trimmed with very broad lace. Lead-coloured gloves. Green fan.

Right-hand seated figure. Demi-gipsy hat, trimmed with green ribands, forming a large bow in the front, and a very small one behind. A narrow white net, plaited round the edge of the brim, its two points tied with narrow green ribands, passing under the ringlets and forming behind a small bow. Two party-coloured feathers on the left side. Hair in easy curls; chignon turned up plain, and the ends returned in ringlets. Chemise of spotted muslin; the sleeves tied in two parts with green ribands. Cross-striped green and white sash. Jonquille-coloured gloves. Yellow shoes.

167

Figure 14   Two Ladies, en Negligé, taking an

Airing in a Phaeton.

First Lady. Head-dress: white stamp-paper hat, trimmed with green riband, and tied down with same. One green and one yellow feather placed on the left side. Green gauze veil. The hair in small curls; plain chignon. Plain calico morning dress with long sleeves, the petticoat trimmed with a narrow flounce. Plain lawn handkerchief. Green sash. Lawn cloak, trimmed with lace and tied behind. York tan gloves. Yellow shoes.

Second Lady. Head-dress: straw-coloured hat, trimmed with orange and purple ribands, and a white lawn handkerchief embroidered in lilac, tied down with a white riband. One lilac and white cross-striped large ostrich feather on the left side. The hair in light curls, and hanging down in ringlets behind, bound with a half-handkerchief tied into a large bow in the front. Chemise of spotted muslin, trimmed with a double plaiting of broad lace round the neck, tied in the front with a lilac riband; short loose sleeves, tied in the middle with the same riband. Lilac-coloured sash, tied behind. Jonquille-coloured gloves and shoes.

The Gallery of Fashion, September 1794

Figure 15   Morning Dresses

White and purple striped sarcenet hat, with an embroidered purple border, trimmed round the crown with a rose-coloured gauze handkerchief, occasionally tied under the chin with a rose-coloured riband. The side hair frizzed into large curls; the hair behind turned up and tied very low with a white rosette. A round gown of muslin with long sleeves, trimmed at the wrists with lace, and tied with rose-coloured ribands. The short sleeves over them, and the border of the gown embroidered in white. Handkerchief of plain lawn put within the gown. Gold ear-rings. Rose-coloured gloves and shoes.

127   French Reception Costume. Artist unidentifiable.
      (This is a three-colour print.)
      From "The Queen," August, 1898

126   Walking Toilettes. By A. Sandoz
      From "The Queen," May, 1897

129 "En Bicyclette"
From "The Young Ladies Journal," 1899

128 Visiting Dresses
From "Le Journal des Dames et des Demoiselles," 1899

Sky-blue beaver hat, trimmed round the crown with a broad purple riband, forming a large bow in front. A large yellow ostrich feather placed behind the bow, inclining forwards. The hair frizzed into small curls; the side hair and the hair behind falling in ringlets upon the neck and back. Festoon necklace of coloured beads. Gold ear-rings. Petticoat of spotted muslin. Lawn handkerchief put within the gown. White and rose-coloured striped chintz gown; short sleeves, with a full cuff of white lawn trimmed at the top and bottom with a broad edging; a plaiting of the same round the neck. Yellow bow placed behind in the centre of the waist. Sky-blue gloves and shoes.

The Gallery of Fashion, November 1794

Figure 16   Two Ladies at Breakfast in their

DRESSING-ROOM

Left-hand figure. Head-dress: a French night cap, a cawl of white muslin, with a double border of lace in white plaits; round the head a broad striped riband quilled, with a large bow behind and in the front. The *peignoir*, or loose jacket, and petticoat of checker muslin, with a very broad hem, and the trimming of plain muslin, scolloped. Large muslin handkerchief within the *peignoir*. A narrow riband tied round the waist. White *mules*, or slippers.

Right-hand figure. Head-dress: *Duke of York's* night cap of clear muslin, the plaits drawn together at the top, and trimmed with a narrow lace, the whole tied round with a small pink riband; deep border edged with the same lace, falling carelessly round the face; a pink riband round the head, tied in a bow behind. Gown and petticoat of fine calico; the petticoat trimmed with a deep flounce of plain muslin; the gown with a capuchin cape, and long sleeves tied at the wrists with pink riband; the whole trimmed with plain muslin. Large muslin handkerchief within the gown. Red morocco slippers.

Figure 23   LONDON FASHIONS, AS WORN IN

DECEMBER 1806

A Morning Dress. Of French cambric, made with a train; plain waist, rather high behind, and sharply rounded at the chest; trimmed round the bottom with muslin *à-la-corkscrew*; long and very full sleeves, edged at the hands with the same; a blue riband round the waist, terminating with bows and ends on the right side. The cap *à-la-cloister*, entirely concealing the hair, flowing loose, and shading the face on the left side, gathered above the right eyebrow in a sort of irregular nosel, and simply confined round the head with a blue riband, and finishing behind with a bow, forms the crown or caul of the cap. A neckerchief, or shirt, sitting full in the front, with a deep falling collar, embroidered at the edge. Limerick gloves and jean shoes.

Mourning Full, or Opera Dress. A Spanish vest and petticoat of Italian crape, worn over white satin, with a rich border of embossed velvet, terminating at the extreme edge with a narrow vandyke or fringe of bugles; the petticoat gathered in a drapery towards the right knee, with a cord and tassels; the front of the vest made high and formed in irregular horizontal gathers, confined with two narrow bands of bugles, terminating at the corners of the bosom, where the vest flows loose, and forms the square bust, which is finished with a pearl or diamond brooch in the centre. A short full twisted or rucked sleeve, bordered at the bottom similar with the vest. The hair in a plain band round the right temple, relieved and terminated by loose curls, which commence on the crown of the head and flow in long irregular ringlets from the left eyebrow, so as to reach the shoulder. A plain lace veil, with slight border, fastened on the crown of the head, falling over the right side of the bosom and reaching below the waist. A pearl or diamond ornament, blended with the hair, over the left eye. Necklace, ear-rings and bracelets to correspond. White kid gloves, white satin shoes. Fan of ebony, inlaid with ivory, and silver mount.

Figure 24   Walking Fashions to be Worn in

December 1808

An antique frock, formed of white or coloured crape muslin, embroidered (for full dress) round the bottom, bosom and sleeves in a border or the silver ivy-leaf and berry, and worn over a white satin slip. For less splendid occasions it is ornamented with lace, let in at its several terminations. It is made high in the neck for the last-mentioned style, with a full rucked collar; but in the former is so constructed as partially to display the back and shoulders. The Highland spencer is formed of double-twill sarcenet, lined throughout with bright amber; the colour, Spanish fly. It is cut low round the throat and finished with a full irregular frill or collar. The waist of the spencer is plain in the front, and rather extreme in length. The scarf is gathered into a silver dash on one shoulder, flowing partially over the back, and one end crossing the figure in front. The whole is trimmed with spotted ermine or a rich silk trimming of Chinese floss. The traveller's cap, formed of the same material as the spencer, is turned up with spotted ermine or full puckered sarcenet, the same as the lining of the scarf. Gloves of York tan, and shoes of dark green velvet with amber-coloured bows.

La Belle Assemblée, December 1809

Figure 25   English Costume; Concert-room

Full Dress

A Polanese dress of green and yellow double-twilled sarcenet, worn over a drapery of rich white lace, with long sleeves; confined at the bosom, the waist and on the arms by topaz brooches; ornamented with silver trimming and tassels; a body and train of yellow satin. A Grecian head-dress, composed of silver-spangled crape and white satin, marked off at the crown by a wreath of green foil, and finished on the left side with a silver cord and tassels, worn with two white ostrich feathers tipped with green. Topaz necklace and ear-rings. Shoes and gloves of pale yellow, white or green. The hair in full, short ringlets.

La Belle Assemblée, October 1810

Figure 26   WALKING DRESS

A pelisse dress of autumnal brown sarcenet, made low in the neck, trimmed down the front and round the bottom with a rich trimming of vandyked white satin, ornamented with silver frogs; the sleeves buttoned on the inside of the arm to correspond with the front of the dress; over the bosom is tied a light white net mantle, scolloped, and ornamented with acorn tassels. White satin bonnet, with a bunch of wheat in front, and short lace veil. Brown sandals and gloves. Green parasol.

Ackermann's Repository of the Arts, October 1811

Figure 27   EVENING DRESS

A round robe of lavender or lilac crape, with full Turkish long sleeve and Roman bodice, worn over an under-dress of white satin. A round tucker of Paris net, edged with antique lace, with cuffs to correspond. Brooch and clasp of pale topaz; neck-chain and cross of the same. Head-dress in the Eastern style, composed of the hair in curls and ringlets, confined in a caul of silver net, fastened with a Chinese pin at the back of the head, and in front with a knot of brilliants. White satin slippers with silver clasp; gloves of French kid; and fan of silver-frosted crape. Occasional scarf of French lace.

Ackermann's Repository of the Arts, September 1812

Figure 28   WALKING DRESS

A Parisian wrapping dress of plain jaconet muslin, or fine cambric, trimmed on each side, round the neck and wrists, with double borders of at the edge, and set on in a novel and beautiful manner, in scollops, every space forming the scollop being elegantly fluted. The flounces are set at equal, but very short distances from each other, and are all headed by a satin *rouleau*, the same colour as the dress. The corsage is laid in small plaits, and fits exactly to the shape. The sleeves are *en gigot*, and have rich lacings *en carreaux*, on the most visible part of the sleeve, in front of the arm; this lacing is of silk cordon, each diamond terminated by a wrought silk button. A double vandyke *collerette*-pelerine falls over the bust, surmounted by a narrow collar of the same; these graceful appendages are of very fine India muslin beautifully embroidered. A transparent hat of white crape, bound with *terre d'Egypte* sarcenet, and ornamented with puffs of the same, mingled with others of celestial-blue; and a superb plumage waving over the left side, consisting of two long white ostrich feathers; the strings of this tasteful hat are celestial-blue, and float loose. The hair, which is much discovered on one side, is arranged in full curls, and no cap is worn over it. A convent cross of white cornelian, dependent from a braid of hair, a purple reticule of *gros de Naples*, with gold spring and chain, a parasol of emerald-green, and slippers of yellow prunella, complete this appropriate and truly elegant dress.

La Belle Assemblée, April 1826

Figure 40　　　　　　　CARRIAGE DRESS

Pelisse of Turkish satin of a bright blue or hyacinthine colour, lined with white sarcenet and fastened in front; the collar square and turned down; the corsage plain and close to the shape, and ornamented on each side with a row of diamonds of the same material as the dress, edged with a narrow satin *rouleau* of the same colour, and united with a satin button. The two rows diverge towards the shoulders and meet in front at the waist where the diamonds unite in pairs and gradually increase in size as they descend; two rows of swansdown adorn the bottom of the dress, between which is an elegant satin scroll. The sleeve is still *en gigot*, but much smaller from the elbow to the wrist, which has three diamond ornaat the edge, and set on in a novel and beautiful manner, in scollops, every space forming the scollop being elegantly fluted. The flounces are set at equal, but very short distances from each other, and are all headed by a satin *rouleau*, the same colour as the dress. The corsage is laid in small plaits, and fits exactly to the shape. The sleeves are *en gigot*, and have rich lacings *en carreaux*, on the most visible part of the sleeve, in front of the arm; this lacing is of silk cordon, each diamond terminated by a wrought silk button. A double vandyke *collerette*-pelerine falls over the bust, surmounted by a narrow collar of the same; these graceful appendages are of very fine India muslin beautifully embroidered. A transparent hat of white crape, bound with *terre d'Egypte* sarcenet, and ornamented with puffs of the same, mingled with others of celestial-blue; and a superb plumage waving over the left side, consisting of two long white ostrich feathers; the strings of this tasteful hat are celestial-blue, and float loose. The hair, which is much discovered on one side, is arranged in full curls, and no cap is worn over it. A convent cross of white cornelian, dependent from a braid of hair, a purple reticule of *gros de Naples*, with gold spring and chain, a parasol of emerald-green, and slippers of yellow prunella, complete this appropriate and truly elegant dress.

La Belle Assemblée, April 1826

Figure 40   CARRIAGE DRESS

Pelisse of Turkish satin of a bright blue or hyacinthine colour, lined with white sarcenet and fastened in front; the collar square and turned down; the corsage plain and close to the shape, and ornamented on each side with a row of diamonds of the same material as the dress, edged with a narrow satin *rouleau* of the same colour, and united with a satin button. The two rows diverge towards the shoulders and meet in front at the waist where the diamonds unite in pairs and gradually increase in size as they descend; two rows of swansdown adorn the bottom of the dress, between which is an elegant satin scroll. The sleeve is still *en gigot*, but much smaller from the elbow to the wrist, which has three diamond ornaments to correspond, placed perpendicularly. The *ceinture* has a highly-wrought gold buckle in front; deep square collerette of British Brussels lace. Cap of white *crêpe lisse*; a bouquet of damask roses on the right side, and others variously disposed. The hair in large curls, arranged to accord with the border of the cap, which is full and of folded *crêpe lisse*. Gold ear-rings and bracelets; gold chain and eyeglass; jonquille-coloured kid gloves and shoes.

La Belle Assemblée, October 1826

Figure 41 HOME COSTUME

Over an undergarment of India muslin, of the most delicate texture, is worn an elegant *déshabillé* robe of celestial-blue, or of sea-green taffeta, without sleeves. The body is made in the Circassian style, and discovers that of the muslin dress underneath plaited *en chemisette*, with a quilling of thread-*tulle* next the throat: the sleeves are of white muslin, and fastened at the wrists with broad bracelets, enriched with cameos and valuable gems; there are no other ornaments on the sleeves. A sash, the colour of the dress, is loosely tied on the left side with a small bow and long ends. At the border of the muslin petticoat, which is nearly a hand's-breadth longer than the coloured robe, is a full *rouleau* of muslin, wound round with a *cordon* of a novel kind in shining cotton. A *rouleau* of silk finishes also the coloured dress next the hem. An Oriental turban of crape or sarcenet, the same tint as the outer robe, and discovering but little of the hair, arranged in curls on each side of the temples, constitutes the head-dress, with a narrow frill of plaited *tulle* under the chin.

La Belle Assemblée, September 1831

Figure 46 FIRST ARCHERY DRESS

A dress composed of changeable *gros de Naples*, green shot with white. The corsage, made nearly, but not quite, up to the throat, fastens in front by a row of gold buttons, which are continued at regular distances from the waist to the bottom of the skirt. The corsage sits close to the shape. The upper part of the sleeve forms a double *bouffant*, but much smaller than is usually worn. This is a matter of necessity, as the fair archer would otherwise cut it in pieces in drawing her bow. The remainder of the sleeve sits close to the arm. The brace, placed upon the right arm, is of primrose kid to correspond with the gloves. The belt fastens upon a gold buckle; on the right side is a green worsted tassel used to wipe the arrow; a green watered ribbon sustains the *petite poche*, which holds the arrows on the left side. A lace collar, of the pelerine shape, falls over the upper part of the bust. White *gros des Indes* hat, with a round and rather large brim, edged with a green *rouleau*, and turned up by a gold button and loop. A plume of white ostrich feathers is attached by a knot of green ribbon to the front of the crown. The feathers droop in different directions over the brim. The half-boots are of green *reps* silk, tipped with black.

Second Archery Dress

A dress composed of white *chaly*, with a *canezou* of blue *gros de Naples*. The front of the bust is ornamented in the hussar style, with white silk braiding and fancy silk buttons; plain tight back. Long sleeve sitting close to the arm, with a half sleeve, *à l'Espagnol*, slashed with white figured *gros de Naples*. A row of rich white silk fringe is brought from the point of each shoulder in front round the back. *Collerette* of white *tulle*, of a novel form, fastened in front by a gold and pearl brooch. The belt fastens with a silver buckle curiously wrought; the accessories correspond in colour with the *canezou*. White *gros de Naples* hat, ornamented with white ostrich feathers, and a gold button and loop. Half-boots of blue kid.

Le Follet Courrier des Salons, August 1832

Figure 48

At Home. The front hair arranged in bands and ringlets. Two folded bows at the crown of the head, sustained by a high gallery shell comb richly cut, and tufts of cinnamon-coloured gauze ribbons, with cut ends; a delicate gold chain and lozenge crosses the brow, *à la Ferronière*. The gown of pale blue jaconet muslin, with full balloon sleeves somewhat above the elbow, and tight lower sleeves. This plate represents a very distinct pattern of the new *manchettes*, made of French cambric or fine Scotch muslin delicately worked. These *manchettes* promise to be as fashionable as such ornaments were three years back. The shape of the present are a new invention, exceedingly becoming to a lady's hand. Each is in two mitre-shaped pieces: one falls over the hand, nearly to the knuckles; the other over the sleeve—the latter is cleft. The bracelets to be worn with the new *manchettes* are complete contrasts to the heavy false jewellery seen to satiety in the last few years. A row of real pearls, of moss agates, or of exquisite enamel, clasped with a small gem for full dress, with lace or blonde *manchettes*. For such as the costume under discussion—"a home dress", a light chain of gold or of hair, is placed at the parting of the two pieces. The corsage of the dress is quite plain, and tight to the bust, cut rounding to the bosom. The skirt likewise plain, gathered round the waist, and a low hem at the bottom. A chemisette of very clear plain net, finished at the throat with a lace ruff, beneath which is tied a cravat of cinnamon-coloured *gros de Naples*, with the ends worked in floss silk of a lighter shade. An apron of silk of the same colour, surrounded by a cord of the colour; and it has corners and pockets, embroidered in lighter cinnamon silk of an acorn pattern in foliage. The apron is tied with a thick cord, and tassels of the same shade. The scarf is of silk muslin, printed in rose-coloured sprigs and pattern, and finished with deep rose-coloured and white fringe. The brodequins are cinnamon *reps* silk and bronze leather. Our fair subscribers will see that we have been elaborate in this description, because it presents many new inventions, and because, after all, the test of an elegant woman is the propriety and delicate finish of an "at home costume".

Child's Dress. Dress of nankeen-coloured jaconet. The corsage *à la vierge*. For walking, a round cape of the same material, with plaited cambric frill and a pink *gros de Naples* cravat. Sleeves tight to the elbow, and round and full above. The trousers are tucked lengthways, and drawn round the ankle with tucked frills. Brodequins, stone-coloured prunella and black.

Le Follet Courrier des Salons, September 1833

Figure 49

Walking Dress. Dress of *gros de Naples, vert de Seine,* the corsage *à la Grecque, à double revers,* or *à pelerine.* The revers is deep on the shoulders, and narrower towards the back and front and is edged with a narrow white blonde. The sleeves are very full at top, and tight from the elbow to the wrist. Skirt put on in full plaits. A *guimpe* of cambric, edged with narrow lace, is worn inside the low body. Hat of crape, ornamented with gauze ribands and two ostrich feathers, placed at the centre of the front. Cravat of black lace, from which a Maltese cross is suspended by a velvet riband. White silk gloves and stockings *à jour.* Black shoes, tied at the back. The sitting figure gives the back of the dress.

Le Follet Courrier des Salons, May 1834

Figure 51

Toilette de Promenade. Dress made *en redingote* of organdi, embroidered down each side of the front *en tablier,* and round the bottom of the skirt above the hem; sleeves *à l'imbécile;* the pelerine, round at back, and reaching to the waist in front, with a large square collar, is trimmed with lace, and embroidered to match the dress. Hat of *paille d'Italie* (Leghorn) ornamented with sarcenet ribbons and feathers. Parasol of *poux de soie,* white silk gloves, open work stockings, and shoes of satin royal.

Le Follet Courrier des Salons, March 1836

Figure 53

Ball Dress. Dress of satin, the corsage made to fit tight to the bust, the front in four pieces, and terminating by a slight point. The sleeves *à triple sabot;* a *revers* or pelerine *decollettée* ornaments the corsage, it is rather deeper on the shoulders than at either back or front, and is trimmed all

180

round with a white silk fringe: a puffing of coloured satin ribbon goes round the bosom of the dress, and is fastened in front by a small bow. On the shoulders are the *nœuds de page*, the ends fringed, the lower part of the sleeves is also trimmed with a silk fringe: this dress made in white crape, is singularly becoming to young ladies, who can vary the colour of the ribbons at pleasure. A graceful trimming of the broadest satin ribbon, fastened at the left side of the waist, crosses the front of the dress, and terminates a little below the knee at the right side of the skirt: this trimming is ornamented with three bows and long ends; a small one at the waist, a second rather larger in the centre, and a third very large below; the ends of the ribbon are fringed. The head-dress consists of a *résille* of satin, the colour of the ribbon on the dress. The back hair is in braids, drawn up to the top of the head, where it is formed into three *coques* or bows. The front hair is in smooth bands as far as the temples, where it falls into long full tufts of curls. A few light bows of ribbon ornament the *résille* at the temples, and a few larger bows are intermixed with the back hair. Gold necklace and ear-rings; long kid gloves, ornamented with a puffing of ribbon, to match the dress. Silk stockings *à jour*; black satin shoes; fan *à l'antique*.

Sitting figure gives back of the dress.

Journal des Demoiselles, August 1853

Figure 74

I now present our fashion-plate to you, and I am convinced that you will find it as charming as I do myself. Let us first examine the young lady seated on the swing.

Her nankeen dress has its corsage and its sleeves adorned with broderie anglaise; a band of muslin has been adapted all round it, and the broderie lies on top of the nankeen and the muslin; naturally, the broderie anglaise is made with white cotton, and that the band, which follows all the contours of the corsage, has to end with a scollop which is more or less open-work. Charming costumes can be made by adorning the front of the skirt and the mantlet in the same way; especially if you set it all off with a hat trimmed with black velvet and kingfishers' feathers.

The other young lady wears a muslin dress, with embroidered bands forming an apron. This is a festoon with a large circle composed of several smaller ones, the corners of the front being similarly embroidered. As for the hat, I have told you the way to make it and the picture will encourage you to begin it. (*Translation*)

Journal des Demoiselles, January 1855

Figure 76

The toilette of the young woman in the foreground is composed of a dress made of antique moiré. The three flounces are adorned with flat feathers, the name of which I am unable to tell you; but they make a charming embellishment, as they can be used in all sorts of ways, both as regards disposition and colour. Several rows of the same feathers are to be found on the bodice and on the sleeves. The chemisette and the sleeves are of Valenciennes lace enhanced with raised satin-stitch—a new and very sumptuous form of embroidery. But I am not speaking either for you or for myself, although the young *lady* in the picture certainly has a right to indulge in this form of elegance. So far as we ourselves are concerned, we can take our share in this costume by substituting taffeta for the antique moiré and replacing the feathers by velvet or fancy braid. (*Translation*)

La Belle Assemblée, July 1864

Figure 90   FULL TOILET DRESS

First Figure. Of spring green, or other coloured silk. The skirt is trimmed with a wide silk band of a darker tint, bordered by a double piping. Body with two points in front, and three behind. Sleeves almost tight, ornamented with a jockey. Puffed *tulle* bonnet, having a loose crown, and ornamented at the side with a cluster of field daisies. A row of English lace falls over the edge of the front on the daisies, which trim the inside. Strings bordered with a fluting of white crape. White moiré antique parasol, ornamented with a chenille fringe.

Second Figure: Toilet for a little girl of four years old. Frock of the new tissue, called "lino", ornamented with black silk braiding on the skirt. Bernese bodice. Chemisette in Swiss plaits. Hat of unbleached rice straw, having the brims lined with pink silk. In front a cluster of roses. Narrow pink velvets round the crown.

Third Figure: Morning toilet for the country. White muslin dress, embroidered in spots, and trimmed at the bottom of the skirt with a plain muslin flounce laid in plaits, and headed with an insertion. Body cut in the Figaro style, and terminated by a short rounded tail. Sleeves almost tight. A Swiss chemisette is worn with this toilet. The body and sleeves in our model were lined with silk of a light tint; but this is a matter of taste. Another very pretty toilet for the country is composed of goat's hair, light grey, with pekin stripes. The skirt is cut into scollops at the bottom, and bound with ponceau silk or cashmere, and a Swiss corselet of the same is worn over a plaited chemisette, with puffed undersleeves, the puffings being divided by insertion. A short round cloak of the same material as the dress, and scolloped and bound to match, is worn with it. Tuscan hat, with a *ponceau* velvet band, forming an aigrette of loops in front, placed at the foot of a black feather.

INDEX

INDEX

The periodicals in this list are mostly referred to by a "short title". The names of the periodicals appear in italics. *Figure numbers* of illustrations are printed in **heavy type**.

188